88 DAYS

BRYON VAN FLEET

PublishAmerica
Baltimore

© 2005 by Byron Van Fleet.
All rights reserved. No part of this book may be reproduced, stored in a retrieval system or transmitted in any form or by any means without the prior written permission of the publishers, except by a reviewer who may quote brief passages in a review to be printed in a newspaper, magazine or journal.

First printing

ISBN: 1-4137-7044-4
PUBLISHED BY PUBLISHAMERICA, LLLP
www.publishamerica.com
Baltimore

Printed in the United States of America

The true story of Clem Pine,
a survivor of the 600-mile
European Death March:

the least known major event of
World War II.

CONTENTS

Acknowledgments	7
Preface	9
Chapter 1: The War That Lasted 40 Seconds	15
Chapter 2: A Flight Crew Is Formed	26
Chapter 3: The Air War Strategy	43
Chapter 4: *The Round Trip* Goes Off to War	53
Chapter 5: Mission Completed	77
Chapter 6: Becoming a POW	87
Chapter 7: Stalag Luft 4	100
Chapter 8: Life in a Prison Camp	113
Chapter 9: The Death March	134
Chapter 10: Fallingbostel	159
Chapter 11: Liberation	173
Epilogue/Author's Comments	176
Bibliography	183

ACKNOWLEDGMENTS

First and foremost I would like to not only acknowledge Clem Pine but thank him sincerely for both the hours he spent with me in production of this manuscript and the untold hours he has spent sifting through his memory—as well as his materials and memorabilia.

I would like to offer a special thanks to Clem's son, Grant, who generously gave me the green light to go ahead with this project, as I know he had considered doing it himself.

The many veterans of World War II who gave me permission to use their stories and offered information so that this story would be told are too many to mention, but I would be remiss if I didn't offer a special thanks to Charles Taylor, George Hood, Hal Goetch, Earl Wassom, and a special veteran from Alabama who wishes to remain anonymous.

The entire history of the European Death March would probably have been lost forever if it were not for the extraordinary efforts of one man, Joseph P. O'Donnell. Mr. O'Donnell has collected hundreds of anecdotes and thousands of facts from veterans scattered all around the country. He has generously provided all of the photographs of Stalag Luft 4 and the death march found in this book.

Thanks also to The Library of Congress for the B-17 photograph.

There are also two understanding wives who put up with the hours Clem and I worked putting this together. Both my wife, Sheryl, and Clem's wife, Ann, were not only patient but outright supportive of the project. Thank you, ladies.

And of course the real "Thank You" must be offered not only to Clem Pine but also to the thousands of young Americans just like him who willingly left their families and homes to fight for our country. Without that effort this book certainly would never have been written. It is with good reason that they have been called "The Greatest Generation."

PREFACE

My wife and I own a used bookstore. In the mid 1990s an elderly gentleman entered the store and asked if I had any World War II books. I directed him to the appropriate section and went about my business with other customers. When there was a lull at the counter, I went to the military section and asked him if I could be of help. His eyes glistened a bit, and in a quavering voice he said, "Do you have anything on the U.S.S. Indianapolis?" My skin grew cold and I dared to ask him, "Sir, were *you* on the Indianapolis?" He quietly answered, "Yes."

I knew the horrible story of the Indianapolis well, and knew what an honor it was to be speaking to one of the few survivors of that doomed ship. Mr. Sherman Booth explained he was looking for books on the tragedy so he could give one to each of his family members, "so they will know."

We had a nice conversation and he explained to me that, until just a few years before, he didn't want to talk about his war experiences and especially the shark-infested horror story that surrounded the sinking of his ship. It was such a typical response that is heard over and over again from the veterans of World War II. These guys won the war, they became "The Greatest Generation," yet when they returned home they set out to build lives, families, and careers, but they never talked much about the war.

Their stories need to be told, and now, in the twilight of their lives, their stories are finally emerging.

Grant Pine, a very good friend of mine, had made comments from time to time that his father had been a B-17 tail gunner over Europe during World War II. From the tone of his comments it was obvious he was proud of his father but it seemed to me that he had the story a bit mixed up, as he said his dad had participated in a "death march."

Like most of us, when I put together "death march" and World War II, I automatically thought of Bataan, and the unbelievably cruel death march that U.S. and Filipino troops suffered at the hands of the Japanese shortly after the start of the war, in April of 1942. However, Grant was *sure* that this death march had been in *Europe* at the *end* of the war and thus began my education into what surely must be the least known major event of World War II, The Nazi Death March.

I probed Grant for more details and he gave me a thumbnail sketch of the story as he understood it, but was apologetic for not knowing more of the details. We both agreed his father's story should be recorded, and after much soul searching, I asked if he would be comfortable with me talking with his father in hopes that we could add this incredible story to the body of knowledge that is World War II.

How lucky was I! Meeting Grant's father, Clem, and getting to know him has been an immeasurable honor. He is one of the warmest, most generous gentlemen I have ever had the pleasure to know. I feel privileged to be the recorder of his story and forever more will treasure those evenings that he and Grant, and I, huddled in his den over the tape recorder and listened as Clem spun out his story. It's been about sixty years now, but

Clem's mind is just as quick as it was in the days he was dueling with Messerchmitts over the Third Reich. He rolls out the story with all the life and animation of a 19-year-old kid in the back of a B-17. His eyes would glisten; his smile would stretch his cheeks, and with no trouble at all Clem would take us back to that air war over Germany. The three of us would be dodging flak together. We were wounded, shot down, bailed out, and suffered POW camp together in that den. Each night when our recording session was over, I was drained.

On our last night, we seemingly joined Clem on the inhumane struggle that would rival any death march soldiers ever endured. Somehow in the warmth of that den the three of us endured frost bight, starvation, filth, lice, and dysentery, as for months and months we struggled through the frozen Polish winter in hopes of liberation.

The session ended and Grant and I went to our homes and nice, warm beds. We left Clem to his inspirational memories and his gut-wrenching dreams. His story, his adventure, his tragedy had been lived out starting when he was just 18 years old and ended when he was only 20, yet this fleeting period of just 33 months had been the defining event of his long, rich life. It is the story of the Eighth Air Force during World War II and the horrendous death march that was endured by tens of thousands, or perhaps hundreds of thousands, of prisoners that had been held by the Germans. These unfortunate souls were of a dozen nationalities and yet this incredible story has seldom been told and only rarely has any mention of it been published. It is, however, a story that should be told. For the sake of history it *must* be told.

I have attempted in this book to weave the personal story of one young man, Clem Pine, into the overall fabric of the air war that was fought by thousands of American, British, and German youngsters. It is a story that for too many ended up with death or the struggle to survive in prisoner-of-war camps and the notorious death march that followed. These young warriors were just in their teens or twenties, but no matter their age or nationality they were all off on the greatest adventure of their young lives. This, then, is that story and how it impacted upon the life of one of the finest Americans I have ever had the privilege to know, Clem Pine.

EIGHTY
EIGHT
DAYS

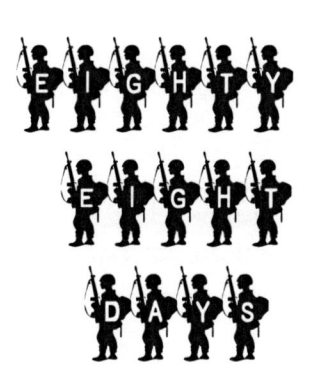

CHAPTER 1
THE WAR THAT LASTED 40 SECONDS

On his previous three flights, Clem Pine, kneeling in the tail of his B-17, had not once fired his twin 50-caliber machine guns. In fact, nobody on this Flying Fortress had had the opportunity to unleash their guns on the dreaded Luftwaffe.

Day after day they had climbed into these enormous silver bombers and lumbered their way across Germany through the incredibly cold, crisp air that envelops the earth at the rarified altitude of 25,000 feet. They had dodged their way through exploding flak shells as they made their devastating bombing runs over German cities, but at this point in the war there were no longer any German fighters to contend with. At least it seemed that way, on the morning of August 16, 1944, as disaster was about to befall some sixty very unlucky American airmen.

It almost smelled as if something was wrong. Things had become just too easy; it was unsettling. Clem knew that despite the lack of "action" the German Messerschmitt 109s, Focke-Wulf 190s, and a myriad of other Luftwaffe hunter-killers were still out there prowling the skies over Germany, just itching to lay waste to these hated American intruders in their bombers. These heavy bombers were daily raining fire, death, and destruction, not only upon the factories of the Fatherland, but upon the homes and neighborhoods as well. The civilians on the ground referred to them as "Chicago Gangsters." The hate was real.

These enormous "Flying Fortresses" absolutely bristled with machine guns, but despite all of their armament they were still vulnerable to the German fighters. The only time they were close to being "safe" was when they were surrounded by escorting American fighters, their "little friends."

This morning they were being accompanied by a very appreciated flight of American P-51 Mustangs. These planes were considered to be the best fighters of World War II. They were extremely fast and had the ability to fly forever without refueling. Well, maybe not forever, as on this morning by about 10 o'clock they were regretfully getting low on fuel and were about to depart for home. The schedule called for them soon to be replaced by an escort group of P-47 Thunderbolts that would accompany the massive bomb-carrying giants on to their target. These Thunderbolts were big, fast planes that from a distance looked a lot like German FW 190s.

On this particular morning these trusted American Thunderbolts would replace the Mustangs and take over the escort duties on to the target, the aircraft factories northwest of Leipzig, Germany, and then stay with the bombers on the trip back to England. So, as it neared the 10 o'clock hour that morning, the Mustangs waggled their wings as a "good-bye" gesture and peeled off heading home to Britain.

In the rear of his plane Pine was engulfed in his electrically heated "underwear" and his heavy leather flight suit, all designed to ward off the extreme cold of 25,000 feet. He could hear his own breathing as he inhaled and exhaled through his life-giving oxygen mask. Up there, in that thin cold air, he wondered about the whereabouts of the scheduled Thunderbolts. They should have arrived by now, but all that was visible in the sky that morning was a heavy blanket of thick, white clouds about 500 feet above Fortress #613, in which he kneeled while scanning the skies. Not just Pine, but everyone in the formation of thirty-seven, now un-escorted bombers, began to get nervous. Just a little at first, and then the tension grew, as the protecting Thunderbolts were nowhere to be seen.

Clem Pine had been on enough missions to feel a distinct discomfort about those thick, white clouds just a few hundred feet above him. There aren't many places to hide a plane in the sky but clouds make a wonderful lair for an ambush. There weren't supposed to be many German fighters left in August of 1944, but if there were any out there today, that would be the perfect place for them to be lurking. The only other place to hide up there is in front of the sun. Even when you're wearing sunglasses or goggles, when a plane comes at you right out of the sun it just can't be seen until it's too late. Every fighter pilot has known that since WWI. Every man in a bomber's crew has known that, too.

As the aloneness set in, the formation approached Eisenach. It was an aloneness that was about to turn into 40 seconds of terror that none of these flyers would ever forget, *if* they were lucky enough to survive. The first sign of trouble was the ugly, black exploding clouds of flack that the Germans were lobbing an amazing 25,000 feet into their formation. There was absolutely no defense against these exploding shells of jagged hot steel, other than luck. Either one of these high altitude cannon bursts hit your plane, or it didn't. You couldn't juke, jink, or dodge like you might if a fighter attacked. You couldn't shoot back, as the German boys on those guns were nearly five miles below you. You could change your altitude, but that was no guarantee of safety, and if you were unlucky it might make things worse. No, you just flew on, thanked your lucky stars, counted your blessings, and said your prayers… and you kept scanning the skies for the Luftwaffe.

And through it all, there was that ominous bank of clouds hanging right over the flight. The formation made a sweeping right turn, away from the sun, as the worried Pine yelled to the ball turret gunner, "Hey, Ponder, look where they're flyin' us." And with that, Pine's premonition came true, as his world turned into a hellish nightmare that would change his life forever.

Joe Nealon, the flight engineer, came over the intercom, his voice relaxing with the relief from their aloneness. "Hey, look, we've got a bunch of P-47s behind us." At last, Nealon thought, the "little friends" had arrived to provide escort for them. "P-47s, shit! Those are FWs," Pine indelicately bellowed into the intercom as his experienced eyes instantly discerned the subtleties between the friendly American P-47 Thunderbolts and the deadly German Focke-Wulf 190s that had erased so many planes of the American Eighth Air Force.

Incredibly, this little snapshot of the air war would last only a short, fleeting forty seconds. But in those forty ticks lives would be ended, bodies would be shattered, and dreams would evaporate. Widows would germinate and parents would be devastated. Medals would be earned and heroes would be created. Most of the airmen would fly home to a warm bed and another beer. However, in just two thirds of a minute, a bunch of American kids, just months out of high school, would have their young lives rudely snuffed out. Others would suddenly be transformed from the carefree youth of America into prisoners of war. Life can be so fickle.

Exactly as Clem had feared, this gaggle of planes had instantly dropped out of the clouds and out of the sun, wingtip to wingtip, with their wings winking. These weren't friendly winks. No. They were the voracious cannon bursts that sent the deadly 20mm cannon shells to eat into the formation of B-17s. The cannon shells had timed fuses and instantly were exploding in angry white puffs throughout the bomber formation. These robin blue, highly polished, beautifully painted Focke-Wulf 190s would have been the prize possession of any aircraft museum director after the war, but here they brought with them more death, destruction and carnage than the 91st Bomb group would see in any other forty seconds of the war.

Just forty seconds. (The entire battle took less time than it takes to read this page.)

Within a few seconds of their startling appearance, the Germans singled out #000, a bomber in the middle of the formation. The pilot, Lieutenant Lindsey, desperately tried to avoid their attack but it was to no avail. Chunks of metal, clouds of gasoline, and pieces of engines and propellers flew erratically off into space as deadly cannon shells shredded his wing. As the entire plane disintegrated into a flaming ball of orange and black, its tail section flew off, still containing the tail gunner, Sergeant Morgan. From its crew of nine, eight men had just perished. Only Morgan survived the initial assault, but he was now plunging five miles earthward, tangled in the wreckage of this elevator that he was rapidly riding to the ground floor. After what seemed a lifetime, he wrestled himself free of the mangled wreckage and kicked open the tail hatch door. The ground was now rapidly approaching and he jumped. He managed to pull the ripcord a mere 600 feet from mother earth. He broke his left heel and leg, but he survived.

Twenty five thousand feet above, the melee had just begun.

Just behind Pine's plane flew #634, *Texas Chubby*. She was jumped and both plane and crew were absolutely perforated from end to end from the exploding cannon shells. The pilot had absolutely no control, as all the instruments and control cables had been shot to pieces. Two of the gunners died in the hail of fire, and the waist gunner had both of his legs blown off by exploding cannon shells. Within seconds *Texas Chubby* exploded, lifting nearby planes (including Pine's) through the air. Airplane chunks flew in every direction, and bodies were thrown all over the sky. One of those bodies belonged to Lt. Gilligan, the co-pilot, who had not yet put his chute on when their fortress exploded. His not-quite-dead body revived as he plunged earthward. Somehow, the parachute he had been about to snap on to his harness when *Texas Chubby* exploded was still clutched in his death grip. As he whistled toward earth his head finally cleared enough for him to recognize the gravity of his situation. He managed to snap his chute onto his body harness and pull the ripcord. He was about to become a POW.

The fate of Sergeant Mis, the tail gunner, was not yet assured. He had struggled to the side hatch when *Texas Chubby* exploded. At least he had attached his chute at the moment the fireball erupted and he was sent flying, but not all of the plane had disintegrated. The entire tail section was now drifting to earth so close to Mis that he was bumping against it as he and this deadly wreckage plummeted downward in tandem. He realized that to pull the ripcord would entangle his chute in this mangled wreckage and reduce his lifetime to the next few seconds. He wisely managed to push off from the tail, drift free and pull the cord. Another POW was created and five more American airmen were dead.

The forty seconds were still ticking.

To the left of Pine's plane, #673: *Lassie Come Home*, was under attack. The exploding cannon shells instantly took the lives of the ball turret gunner, the radio operator, the navigator, and the co-pilot. The interior was a blazing inferno and the left wing was aflame. The five living members bailed out, but the scene that will never be forgotten by those who witnessed it was that of the flapping body of a dead crewmember that was wedged halfway out of the flaming mess as it sailed to the earth. *Lassie* did not come home.

Tick, tick, tick. Just forty seconds.

To the left rear of Pine's position, #996: *Boston Bombshell* was becoming the victim of yet another savage attack. As the fighters pounced on the bomber, all four of its engines exploded in flames. Immediately the plane began to spin earthward. Those who could do so, bailed out, and immediately thereafter *Boston Bombshell* exploded in a massive fireball. Two crewmen managed to drift to earth alive. Of the other seven, three were mercifully killed in the attacks or explosion. The remaining four made it out of the burning wreckage but had been ensnared in the flames. As they pulled the ripcords, their flaming chutes popped open and left them suspended several miles above the earth beneath burning parachutes. Within moments all four were plunging those five miles to oblivion. In this forty second war it was not yet halftime.

Lt. Fonke's plane, #012, collapsed under the initial assault. This powerful Flying Fortress was simply torn to pieces by cannon shells. Two men were dead and seven others frantically struggled to just get out any way they could. As they left their shattered Fortress it exploded sending men and wreckage all over the sky. Five planes had now been destroyed but this angry little chapter of the war was still not over.

In front of Clem's bomber flew Lt. Leslie's #126. Within seconds a Focke-Wulf had sent cannon shells into and through #126. The Germans had come up under Pine's plane so close that the pilots of the two planes could see each other. The attacker began to "walk his rudder," a maneuver that sprayed cannon shells back and forth, tearing Leslie's bomber to bits. Chutes began to appear as crewmen dived out of their plane. Lt. Leslie stayed with the plane, trying all the time to regain control until it exploded. Three men perished in that explosion but six others were floating to earth. Second Lieutenant Stanley Koss managed to land safely only to be shot and killed by an angry old man as he landed. Sergeant Godfrey also landed intact and was about to be killed by a crowd with pitchforks when a little seven-year-old girl stepped in front of him, spread her arms in defiance, and the angry mob backed down. For saving his life Sergeant Godfry gave her the only thing he could think of at the moment, his sticks of gum.

Six planes were down.

The forty ticks were about to abruptly end for Clem Pine.

Clem had been kneeling on pads, with his butt on a bicycle type seat and scanning the skies when the Focke-Wulfs dropped right out of those clouds. Just to his left lay his parachute. There wasn't enough room for him to wear it in the cramped tail of his B-17, and amazingly enough, neither he nor any of these other bomber crewmembers had actually been trained how to use it. Oh, they had instructions on how to snap it on, and how to land, but none of them had ever actually made a parachute jump.

The instant he recognized these predators as Focke-Wulfs, and had shouted it to his crew, Clem sent a double stream of 50-caliber machine gun shells into their path from his twin guns. On previous missions he had shot down several German fighters and was considered to be a highly prized crewmember. He had good eyesight, fine aim, and nerves of steel. As he opened fire, they did, too. Their wings just kept on winking as those 20mm cannon shells tore into this formation of bombers. It was a terrifying moment as one of those cannon shells ripped into the tail of Clem's plane with a thunderous explosion. The tail of #613 turned into chaotic horror. The deafening detonation blew Clem's parachute to shreds and tore a yard-long chunk out of the tail section itself. Being in the epicenter of this mayhem, Pine's body was riddled with ragged shrapnel chunks. His left leg was imbedded with steel fragments, and his right wrist was lacerated and bleeding profusely. The explosion destroyed his intercom link to the rest of the plane and his oxygen system was obliterated. He should have been killed.

How all of this happened, Clem never knew, because the violence of that cannon shell exploding in his tiny compartment had instantly thrown his body some ten feet back through the fuselage of the now crippled plane. Clem shouted, "My God, I've had it," and passed out.

During the attack, not only had Clem Pine been shot up, but as those cannon shells raked up the fuselage of his plane, one of them hit Clayton Tyson, the waist gunner. Tyson was "a real nice kid" and hadn't been married long. The shell instantly blew off the back half of his head, leaving his crumpled body piled up just behind Clem.

The cannon shells continued their deadly march right up the plane, leaving a gaping hole in the leg of the radio operator, Gerald Peters, and then they proceeded to blow out the Plexiglas nose above the bombardier, which caused papers, maps, and anything loose to be sucked right on out into space. Finally, in this three or four seconds of death and destruction, the number two engine was knocked out and the plane started losing altitude rapidly. Flying fortress #613 was doomed.

Who knows how long Clem Pine lay there, with no oxygen mask, in the rarified air at 25,000 feet, but after some time he came to. That in itself was probably a miracle, as anoxia easily sets in at that altitude. In his training, Clem recalled someone had once said that if you pass out once at this altitude you might wake up, but if you then pass out a second time, you'll never wake up again. Clem was dizzy. Clem was wounded. For the first time in his war, Clem Pine was truly scared. He could see his friend Tyson was dead, and Peters was standing there with a hole in his leg, and the plane was headed down. After seeing the carnage of six planes exploding all around him it was only too obvious that his plane was about to disintegrate in a fireball, too. His chute was shredded. What was he to do? He had to exit that great wounded bird and it better be fast. Panic set in. Clem Pine was certainly a true hero in every sense of the word, but he was also just one scared kid. He had just turned 20.

As #613 careened down, with his head still dizzy he recalled that on an earlier flight one of the air war veterans had recommended to him that he take an extra parachute and place it behind some bungee cords next to the main door, "just in case." Praise the Lord. If ever there was a "case" this was surely it. The forty seconds were over. Without a second thought, Clem snapped that chute onto his chest, kicked open the door and left.

What Clem Pine left was the worst forty seconds of terror the 91st Bomb Group would ever experience. He left some of the best friends he had ever had. He left that life in the barracks, with the stories and the jokes and the letters from home. He left England and the pubs, and the beer, and the girls, and the good times. He left the only life he had ever known. He also left the intense noise of his twin machine guns in that little tail. He left the noise of those cannon shells blowing his plane apart, and he also left the noise of those six B-17s all blowing up within the last forty seconds. It was eerily quiet.

His parachute opened with a "pop" as this carnage was going on all around and above him. As he hung there in that chute, he could see all those planes, all those "buddies," flying away with out him. He was all alone. His only companions were the other parachutes scattered about the sky with whom he would spend the next ten minutes drifting down into Nazi Germany, into the Third Reich, into POW camps, and into who knows what. His first thought was for his mother. "Oh shit! My mother's gonna be frantic," thought that scared kid as he hung there in his parachute.

What Clem Pine did not know was that his pilot, Flight Officer Marpil, would fight the controls of his wounded #613 down to about 14,000 feet and turn for home all alone. He would get hit repeatedly by anti-aircraft fire and continue to lose engines. As he reached the coast of England the last engine died and he made a dead stick landing in the grass. The plane was damaged beyond repair but it had made it home. Without Clem Pine.

CHAPTER 2
A FLIGHT CREW IS FORMED

As Clem Pine drifted into this frightening new world below him, his thoughts ricochet from his friends in the bomber, to his mother in California, and then to his very survival in the hostile world that was fast approaching. He had been taught it was the civilians he had to worry about. They were much more ruthless to flyers than the police or soldiers. Numerous accounts had been told how angry mobs had shot, hanged, or beaten flyers to death. Would friendly farmers spare his life, or would this short life of just twenty years end abruptly at the hands of an angry mob?

It hadn't been a particularly unusual twenty years. He was a perfectly normal American boy who had come of age in the Great Depression. He had been born in Montana but had spent his youth bouncing back and forth between California and Montana, living with relatives. He had known what it was to have no money, no job, no home. Oh, he had a "home" created by a loving mother and five older siblings, and even a caring father who was sometimes around. But he had never had that stability of growing up in one community, with long-term friends, the same school, the same teams, and the real roots that create a "Hometown." But being born in 1924 and growing up in the depression there was nothing unusual about bouncing around from location to location, trying to find a way to make ends meet. An *ordinary American boy* would pretty much describe the young Clem Pine who was about to be dragged into World War II, like so many others of his generation. He dropped out of school at fifteen, bought a car for twenty-nine bucks, and found a hard-to-get job at the *San Francisco News* working as a "mailer." He had a crummy old bolt-action 20-gauge shotgun that he would take duck hunting on his days off, but he was a lousy shot. There was nothing at all noticeably remarkable about this typical American kid.

Events were about to change his world, and not just Clem's world, but the entire world. Like so many of his generation he was about to grow quickly into a man. From this larval kid from California would emerge an adult who would need every scrap of courage he could muster, just to survive this war. Clem Pine was about to become a true American war hero. Bravery, courage, loyalty, and patriotism would be kneaded into this ordinary young man and the result would be an airman who would help win a war. The result would be a man that oh so many would be proud to call "my crew-member," "my friend," "my father," "my son," or "my husband."

On that carved-into-your-mind-forever moment of Sunday morning, December 7, 1941, a seventeen-year-old Clem Pine was sitting at the table with his mother and brother, having an early lunch, when the radio stopped their digestive processes on the spot. We were at war. It was time to join up. All over America young men flocked to the recruiting stations to sign up. That is, young men who were at least eighteen years old were signing up. If you were younger you could join if your parents would sign for you, but Mother Pine had other thoughts about what was best for her youngest child. Friends joined, brothers joined, but the seventeen-year-old Clem had to wait until June 27 of 1942 to become eighteen and sign for himself.

After a young man makes the monumental decision to go to war, the next big decision is what branch of the military to join. What would he like to do? Clem liked horses. In fact, Clem loved horses. When he was a kid, he had hung around the Presidio just to watch the cavalry soldiers charge around on their horses as they practiced their maneuvers. Gosh, that seemed so exciting; to be charging into battle, with your saber gleaming in the sun as you cut a swath through those Nazis, or maybe you would be laying waste to the very "Japs" who had bombed Pearl Harbor. Yes, the decision to join the cavalry was easy for Clem. So in the summer of 1942 Clem Pine presented himself to the Army recruiter and proudly announced that the branch of the service he would like to join was the cavalry! One can only imagine the humiliation, the embarrassment, the disappointment, when the recruiting sergeant looked him in the eye and announced, "Son, there are no longer any horses in the cavalry, it's now mechanized!" What? No horses? Clem was shocked at first but soon the shock turned to insult as the recruiter suggested maybe he could get into a mule battalion. Mules! No way! Thus faded the glorious dreams of Clem Pine. Life can be so cruel when you are just eighteen.

Clem had taken the standard battery of tests that all recruits must take, so as he stood there trying to deal with his horseless future the sergeant commented, "You've got some pretty decent scores, son, why don't you go into the Army Air Corps?" Wow! The Air Corp was *almost* as exciting as the cavalry, so that was it. In no time at all Clem found himself at the Presidio Monterey, hoping to be a pilot. He had a friend who had graduated from college and was accepted as an air cadet. Clem was envious of him but the Army Air Corps had other plans for an eighteen-year-old high school drop out. They put him on a troop train and shipped him to Jefferson Barracks, Missouri. The troop train was fun. Civilians along the way would bring sandwiches and drinks to the soldiers. There were cards to be played, songs to be sung, and lies to be told.

At Jefferson Barracks the men were assembled and they started calling out names, telling everybody what discipline they had been assigned to. "Jones, artillery. Johnson, infantry," and so on. Clem finally got up the nerve to ask what was going on. The sergeant explained the procedure and Clem announced, "You can't do that, I'm in the Air Corps."

"Bullshit," bellowed the sergeant. "You're in the Army, man, you'll go where they tell you to go."

"That really scared me," Clem would later say. He had no desire at all to go running around on the ground, and as he had heard they were looking for aerial gunners he volunteered right then and there for aerial gunnery school.

By September of 1942 Clem was off to the Las Vegas Gunnery School. In those days Las Vegas really wasn't much of a town, not that it mattered, for Clem never got a pass the entire time he was there. But Clem didn't need a pass. What he needed was to develop the skills that would keep him and his nine fellow crewmembers alive in the Luftwaffe-filled skies of Nazi Germany. When he arrived he had never seen a B-17 and it is probable the same was true for all of these green kids who just a few months before had been sitting in a high school math class. No "air war" had ever been fought before. World War I had no real bombers. The Battle of Britain had been fought a couple of years before in 1940, but the German bombers and tactics would never amount to anything compared to the bomber trains of B-17s and B-24s the Eighth Air Force would soon be sending over Germany.

A B-17 was well named. It truly was a "Flying Fortress," absolutely bristling with machine guns from every orifice in the plane. It had a man at the machine guns in the nose, another in a top turret, another in the belly turret, a couple of waist gunners and one lonely soul in the rear of the plane manning the tail guns. In a matter of months, these kids (and keep in mind, that's all they really were, just kids) would be packed into these enormous bombers. The bombers, several hundred of them, would be arranged into tight formations and sent over Germany at about 250 miles per hour. Coming at them, in the opposite direction, or maybe from above, or below, or behind, or out of the sun, or out of the clouds, would be hunter-killer packs of Messerschmitt 109s or Focke-Wulf 190s doing about 350 mph. There might be a relative closing speed of over 600 mph! These kids, who would soon be air crewmen, would need to learn to fire their belching, bucking 50-caliber machine guns from a moving airplane that was bouncing through the skies at these moving enemy planes coming from who knows where, that were twisting and turning every which way. They would need to lead their targets the way a duck hunter does. As the bombers flew in such a tight formation Clem and the boys would have to be very careful or they would shoot down one of their own planes, or as happened too often, they might even shoot up their own wings or tail. To swing these machine guns freely the plane had to have open "windows," so being five miles high the wind would be whistling through the plane at minus 50 degrees

Fahrenheit. Therefore, the crewmen would be bundled up in electric underwear, heavy leather flight suites, oxygen masks, and gloves, while trying to calculate angles, distances, and range. To top it off, these "targets" out there were trying as hard as humans can, to kill *you* first!

A large group of bombers, flying tight formations so their gunners could interlock in a defensive crossfire, might have five hundred of these "kids" manning the machine guns. This was designed to be one interdependent unit so that every person and every plane was dependent on the skills of every other plane and every other gunner. If just one guy was "asleep at the switch" it could easily cost the lives of everybody on his plane. And just six months ago these same kids were getting sent to the principal's office for chewing gum in math class, smoking in the bathrooms, or tossing spit wads. A few of the "older" guys were 19 or 20 but almost nobody was old enough to buy a beer or vote. It was as if your local high school was sending the senior class to go and defeat the Nazis.

There was a lot of training to do.

Nobody was exactly sure just how to go about training all these kids for a job that had never been done before. As Clem arrived at aerial gunnery school in early September of 1942, the Americans were just starting to use B-17s to bomb Germany so his instructors were not grizzled old veterans who had years of experience as aerial gunners. Most of them were representatives of ammunition and fire arms companies who had not been to war. They had never taken a shot at the Luftwaffe but they had plenty of experience shooting at ducks in the bayous of Louisiana, or the grain fields of the mid-west, so they brought out shotguns and soon had the boys blazing away at clay pigeons. The trainees did a lot of trap and skeet shooting with 12-gauge shotguns as the instructors kept score.

From being a lousy shot at those ducks in California, Clem soon developed an eye for speed, distance, angles, and all of the complex calculations one must make to hit a fast-moving clay pigeon. Presumably these were the same skills he would need to shoot down enemy fighters. But shooting down those enemy planes was not done while standing firmly on the ground but rather from your own moving airplane, so the next step was to put the trainees in the back of a moving truck that drove around a track while clay pigeons flew in all directions. The boys in the back would blaze away at these moving targets, from their moving truck, as they went 'round and 'round the track. It was a lot of fun. After all, these targets weren't shooting back!

If your scores were high enough you were then presented with your final exam. The exam consisted of climbing into the rear seat of an AT6, a two-seat training plane that would fly along while a nearby plane towed a large mesh sleeve through the air. Your job was to blast away at the sleeve with a 30-caliber machine gun. This was exciting stuff. Clem had never even been up in a plane before, so he listened carefully as the pilot instructed him in all of the intricacies of this "final exam." They would fly along with Clem wearing a parachute, and strapped into the back seat with his seat belt. As the target sleeve approached, Clem was to remove his seat belt and clip himself onto two straps, one on either side that would support him in the standing position in this open cockpit. He then had 100 rounds of ammunition to fire from his moving plane at the moving sleeve towed some distance off to the side. When he used up his ammunition he was to waggle the gun around, which would signal his pilot that he was through. The pilot told Clem that upon seeing this waggle signal he would then "peel off."

The trouble was, Clem, having never flown before, had no

idea what it meant to "peel off." The further trouble was that nobody had told Clem that he should sit back down and strap himself in before he gave the waggle signal. Sure enough, when the still-standing Clem Pine gave the waggle, the pilot peeled off. Clem was left hanging out of the plane, screaming like a banshee and sure he was about to die. The pilot then pulled up the plane, which body slammed Clem back into the seat, and at long last he fastened his seat belt. A visibly shaken 18-year-old Clem Pine climbed out of the plane, having just had his first airplane ride. He had passed his final exam and he was promoted to sergeant. He also had survived aerial gunnery school.

By mid October of 1942 it was off to Salt Lake City to armament school. He spent four weeks learning to strip guns right down to their individual parts. There were lessons about the various types of bombs and their fuses. It was an intensive crash course about the weapons of the air war being fought over Europe. Clem excelled and finished school, graduating with honors, qualified to be the armorer on a B-17. He was thrilled.

The next step on his march to war was Boise, Idaho. In Boise, two major events dominated. The first was the introduction of The Crew. Here, crews were assembled that would go off to war together. These other nine guys would become the most important people in his life. By the time World War II ended and the stories were told, the one theme that was repeated over and over again was the importance of the small fighting unit. It didn't matter what branch of the service men were in, the story was the same. The motivating factor for most of the fighting men was not to defeat the Nazis, nor was it to defend freedom and the American way of life. No, the overriding motivation for nearly every soldier in the war was to not let down their buddies. "You depended on them for your life and they depended on you," was a sentiment that was repeated over and over again. The bonding in most small units was so intense that these men would become the best friends they would ever know and they would remain so for the rest of their lives. For Clem Pine it all started in Boise.

The second major event in Boise was the issuance to Clem of his leather flight jacket. Pride. Yes, Pride with the capital "P" was issued along with that leather jacket. Swagger came along with it. Cockiness came along with it, too. It was a unique uniform issued only to airmen and it probably had a lot to do with the bonding that this group of ten was to know so well. The flight jackets, the togetherness, the dependency, the camaraderie that would carry Clem Pine through the war, all started right here. Clem's leather flight jacket was his most prized possession up until that day in August of 1944 when he bailed out of his crippled B-17 over Germany and left that jacket back in England, never to be seen again.

Along with bringing the crew together, this first phase training in Boise was mostly for the benefit of the pilot. It was his introduction to B-17s and he flew the crew around the area under the watchful eye of an instructor pilot while the rest of the crew familiarized themselves with this magnificent new airplane and its workings. The navigator and flight engineer began to get the feel of things, too, but it was really the pilot who now was learning a set of skills that ten lives would depend on. If he couldn't fly that plane tight in a formation, or efficiently so it didn't waste fuel, he and all of his crewmembers would never make it home. History was about to show that only a small percentage of these aircrews would actually make it through the war, so pilot training was critical.

The crew moved on to Redmond, Oregon, so the bombardier and gunners could take their turn at training.

Mostly they dropped sand-filled bombs at targets in the desert, and the gunners shot at targets on the ground. Clem Pine and the rest of the gunners were about to go off to war, having shot only 300 rounds from the air at other airborne targets! One evening, in the middle of winter, after having completed a training bomb run, Clem's crew was about to meet its first crisis. For some reason the number two engine, the one right next to the plane on the left side, began to "windmill." It appeared that the drive shaft to the propeller had broken. The engine was shut off but the air passing over the plane caused the propeller to spin at a terrific speed. The danger was that upon landing the propeller might just fly off, and due to the direction of rotation it might just come slicing through the plane, probably killing everyone on board in a big fireball. Clearly this group of teenagers, with 22-year-old officers, had never before had to deal with such a life-threatening situation. It got darker and darker as they circled Redmond, trying to decide if they should ride this plane down or if they should just bail out into the wintry night of Oregon. Amazingly enough, for all of the training these guys were getting, they had no parachute training other than how to strap one on and how to pull the rip cord. To jump out alone into that darkness was not a desirable option, so they circled on and on. Finally it was decided they were all in this together and they would all ride the crippled ship down as a unit. Whatever happened to one would happen to all. As they approached the runway everyone hunkered down, held their breath, made plans to bolt from the flaming wreckage, and silently said their prayers. As power was being cut to the other three engines, the whine of the wind-milling propeller reverberated through the plane. They reduced power, dropping lower and lower until finally the squeal of tires hitting the runway could be heard. Everyone waited for the propeller to come smashing through the plane but the big bomber rolled to a stop and ten guys simultaneously let out a sigh of relief. Cohesiveness, bonding, and camaraderie got a big boost that evening. An aircrew was being born.

While in Redmond a change was made that Clem credits for saving his life. The pilot on the crew was not flying as well as the air corps demanded so he was pulled from the crew and held back for further training. A new pilot was assigned to the crew. His name was Henderson Cagle. Cagle instantly gained the confidence of the crew. He stood about 6'2", had a beautiful mustache, and a bundle of confidence. He brought with him many hours of twin engine flying experience from civilian life so it could instantly be seen that here was a real pilot. Cagle could fly! It would turn out that Cagle's ability to keep the plane tucked up in tight formation and not wander all over the sky would bring this plane home, time and again, when things got tough and losses were high. He would become the father figure; after all, he was an "old man." He was 28.

With Cagle at the controls the crew next moved to Pierre, South Dakota, where the navigator could take his turn at practicing. They flew long distances all over the United States to simulate the long missions into Germany that would be in their future. There wasn't much for the rest of the crew to do on these long flights so they gathered in the radio room to play cards and swap tales. Cagle also would now invite the rest of the crew to come forward and take control of the plane. For a couple of hours at a time each crewman would fly the plane, for it was well known by now that, in combat, all of the members of the crew were equally vulnerable to being shot and killed, even if the plane was not shot down. A German fighter might attack head on and kill both the pilot and co-pilot, so it was imperative that someone could fly the plane at least well enough to get them back over England where as a last resort they could bail out, even if landing a B-17 was beyond their flying ability. They also had a chance to learn something about everyone else's job on the airplane. They learned to share responsibilities. They learned about each other. They were growing together as an aircrew.

It must have helped that they were also developing senses of humor. While in training, Clem had noticed that the rudder controls happened to be right over his head. When his good friend Tom Petersen, the co-pilot, was flying he would sometimes put his feet up on these rudder controls and give a little shove so that Petersen would have to trim up the plane. As soon as he got it trimmed Clem would take his feet off the rudder controls and of course the plane would drift out of trim. He got a big kick out of driving Petersen crazy this way. But Petersen had his own sense of humor, too. On these long flights from South Dakota it would sometimes require these guys to relieve themselves and there was no toilet on board. They had a "relief tube" in the radio room but it wasn't very practical, as using it would spew urine all over the ball turret hanging under the plane. Frozen urine didn't seem to be very funny to Joe Lodge, the ball turret gunner. The other option was a simple bucket with a bag in it that could be used if you could balance on it while the plane bounced through the air. If someone had to use the bucket and Petersen was at the controls you could bet he would jerk, juke and shake that airplane any way he could to knock the poor guy off the bucket. The crew found this to be hilarious, but finally Cagle would snap and shout, "Stop it, stop it!" There would then be a good bit of snickering as the poor guy using the bucket went about cleaning up his mess.

Upon finishing this last phase of training each man had had a chance to practice his specialty. There really was nothing left to do but go off to war. Hours and hours had been spent building this aircrew into a fighting unit. They knew their own jobs, they knew each other's jobs, and by now they knew each other. They had become an aircrew.

On March 12, 1943, they headed to Kansas to pick up a brand new B-17. This was to be the plane that would carry them through the war. If they all had mastered their skills, worked together as a team, and had a good portion of luck, they would fly twenty-five bombing missions over Europe. Twenty-five was the magic number. Very few crews would survive all twenty-five missions, but if they did, they had fulfilled their duty and would be rotated back to the States.

One can only imagine the sense of excitement, the feeling of adventure, and the fear of war, that these ten "kids" must have felt as they picked up this beautiful airplane that was to take them off to do battle with the Germans. They knew only that their first destination was Palm Beach, Florida. Their immediate need was to christen the big bird with an appropriate name. All sorts of suggestions were batted around. Cagle, being from Arkansas, leaned toward *Arkansas Traveler*, but Cagle was wise enough not to bully his crew and he let everybody put a name in a hat. From the hat was drawn *The Impatient Virgin*. So that was it, these ten young men and their beautiful *Virgin* were now all set to go off to war.

The usual route to Europe did not run through Florida, it ran up to Newfoundland and ended in Scotland, so there was anticipation in the air as to the whereabouts of their final assignment. To add to the mystery, the suspense, the intrigue of their "secret" mission, their orders were sealed in a special envelope that was not to be opened until they had left Palm Beach and were airborne. To top it all off, the bombardier was made a special finance officer and was given a huge satchel of cash so he could act as paymaster while the boys were off on their international adventure. The atmosphere was filled with excitement as the orders envelope was opened and they were told they were on their way to Africa. Africa wasn't their first choice. They all wanted to go to England, but the plan laid out before them was surely a more exotic trip than any of these ten young men had ever dreamed of. They were part of a unit known as "Major Dejohns Provisional Group" but they were not to fly as a group, but rather this solo plane was to fly all alone to Puerto Rico, then on to Brazil, West Africa, up across the Sahara Desert and the Atlas Mountains to Marrakech Morocco, and finally on to Oran in Algeria.

The excitement ran high.

The first leg to Puerto Rico was uneventful, but there were twenty wide eyes soaking up that glorious blue of the Caribbean as the adventure began. They spent the night in barracks leaving two men to guard the plane. The pair took turns with one sleeping in the plane while the other walked the wings with a sub-machine gun. The next day they were off to Belem in Brazil. Now was the time you trusted that those cross-country flights to acquaint the navigator with his duties would pay off. It's over a two-thousand-mile flight from Puerto Rico to Belem so it was with much relief that the Amazon Basin yielded the airstrip in the jungle. The next day they flew farther south to the Brazilian city of Natal. They were flying low now and as they skimmed over the jungles the entire crew was captivated by the villages as well as the villagers. The fascination was mutual, as the natives would emerge from their houses to watch this magnificent silver bird pass overhead.

The adventure was on.

In Natal the plane had a thorough going over as the next step was across the Atlantic. This gave the crew a day at the beach.

Some of these kids had never seen a beach much less one with the warm waters of equatorial Brazil. It was a day to remember. For some of the crew it was also a night to remember as well. Clem's behavior that night was such that Mother Pine would have approved. Perhaps the same could not be said for the mother of the tail gunner. The white sand beaches, the tropical breeze, and the native girls all led to a night of romance. Perhaps he was just an "impatient virgin." By dawn there had been enough romantic activity that the tail gunner had caught "something." By the time they reached their destination he had a burning in his groin that had become serious enough that the air corps pulled him from the plane. This left the position of tail gunner open. Clem had always coveted that spot but he had been trained to be the plane's armorer, which meant that his job was to be a waist gunner. After some negotiating Clem landed the tail gunner's spot and a new waist gunner would join the crew.

They were now in Dakar, Senegal. This was really Africa, the "Dark Continent" of Stanley and Livingston, of Tarzan, of lions and elephants. Perhaps there were even cannibals! The concern of the air corps, however, was the crossing of the Sahara Desert. Here the plane got checked and rechecked. The twelve hundred miles of the desert were unforgiving. If you went down and the crash didn't kill you the heat would. The only reason the heat might not kill you was that if they could catch you, the locals would kill you first. This was not a place for mechanical troubles, so the *Impatient Virgin* got quite a check-up before she headed north.

Clem recalls that flight as one of the most memorable of his life. The wide vistas of shimmering heat as they crossed the Sahara, the ruggedness of the Atlas Mountains, and then the descent into Marrakech were all seared into his brain for a lifetime.

Just imagine ten kids from Middle America being dropped into Marrakech, Morocco in 1943. They wandered through the bazaars and market places. They stared at the camels and the donkeys. There could hardly have been a more exotic culture on the face of the earth. They stuck together! They were an aircrew.

As it turned out, while making the risky crossing of the Sahara, they had indeed developed mechanical trouble, they just didn't know it. Once they were in Morocco the ground crew diagnosed the engine trouble and grounded the plane until all was put right. This meant they had several more days in Marrakech than had been planned for. Sometimes Lady Luck just throws you a seven.

In England at this time the Eighth Air Force was being developed into a major component of the air war. As its numbers grew, The Mighty Eighth continued to lose planes over Europe, and even lost some in training accidents, so replacements were needed. The obvious place to find them at that time was Morocco. As it turns out the *Impatient Virgin* had been destined to join the Fifteenth Air Force in Italy but now she was given new orders to fly north to England and fill in for one of the planes lost by the Eighth. This was good news. Soon they were off for a night flight to England but things had changed. For the first time in their lives they loaded their guns. They were playing with the varsity now and at any moment they might be jumped by German fighters. As it turned out the flight was uneventful, but the tension on the plane that night told everyone on board that now they were playing for keeps.

On April 19, 1943, these ten young men in their beautiful *Virgin* arrived in England. They had left Kansas on March 6th for what had been the adventure of a lifetime. The trip to

Florida, Puerto Rico, Brazil, Senegal, Morocco, and on to England had been the most exciting adventure any of them had ever experienced. That would soon change.

The Crew of *The Round Trip*.

Top Row, Left to Right: Henderson Cagle (pilot), Tom Peterson (co-pilot), Clem Pine (tail gunner), James Dunn (navigator), Gus Markert (waist gunner), James Fall (radio operator).

Bottom Row, Left to Right: Chester Kinsey (waist gunner & assistant engineer), Al Feldstein (bombardier), Joe Lodge (ball turret gunner), Buss Cartwright (engineer & top turret gunner).

CHAPTER 3
THE AIR WAR STRATEGY

A B-17 over its target.

When Clem arrived in England in April of 1943 the air war was in a state of flux. In fact, it had been in a state of flux from the outbreak of war in 1939. More correctly, the state of war has probably been in flux since mankind had its first war in our distant club wielding past. Side "A" comes up with a technological innovation that gives it an advantage, so side "B" devises a strategy to defeat this new technology. Perhaps side "B" now has gained an advantage so there is a new counter strategy from side "A," and so on. This back and forth flow of technologies and strategies for the air war commenced for the British with the Battle of Britain. Hitler was determined to break the back of the British by his unrelenting destruction of British cities, British armament factories, and British morale. His bombers certainly rained fire and destruction all over Britain. They destroyed buildings, factories and lives, but they never destroyed the morale, the spirit, or the determination of the British people. Time and again the British sent up a few handfuls of very young men in their Spitfires and Hurricanes to defeat Hitler's Luftwaffe. By the end of 1940 Hitler had suffered sufficient losses without breaking the back of Britain, that he withdrew his air force and, with it, his plans to invade Britain. It was this legendary defense of the home country by these few British boys that inspired Winston Churchill to growl out his famous compliment that, "Never in the field of human conflict was so much owed by so many to so few." Yes, the boys flying for the Royal Air Force had proven that they could defeat an armada of invading bombers. They at least could make the cost of the bombing so high that it just didn't make military sense.

It was time for side "B" to devise a new strategy.

Despite this German failure to subdue Britain with aerial bombardment, Air Chief Marshal Arthur "Bomber" Harris was convinced that with the correct tactics the Nazi war machine could be destroyed from the air. The British had failed at pinpoint bombing and soon became convinced that the high altitude bombing of specific targets such as a factory or a ship was impractical. It just didn't work. Harris began to study the devastating raid the Germans had made on Coventry in November 1940. Their target had been industrial centers, but in effect they simply carpet-bombed the city, devastating the infrastructure of power and water systems and destroying so many homes that the workers who operated the industrial plants became "dehoused." Harris soon discovered that it was the fact that so many workers were dehoused, and their lives disrupted, that crippled Coventry's war production, not the destruction of the industrial sites. Thus a strategy was born. Side "B" was about to change its tactics.

The British attempt at strategic bombing started out with small numbers of bombers. In fact, the Americans had sent the British some B-17s in 1941 and the results were disastrous. The B-17 appeared to be a poor design because most of them were badly shot up, and many were not returning from missions at all. The British sent them off in groups of two or three. The basic concept of these heavy bombers had been to amass them in huge groups so that any fighter that would approach them would come under fire from *all* of the planes. The concentrated firepower of so many planes unleashed all at once would overwhelm enemy fighters. After all, there was a good reason they named the plane, *The Flying Fortress*. But in small formations the "forts" were being shot down. The British soon learned that the most successful tactic was to amass large numbers of bombers, not only so they could concentrate their firepower but also so they could overwhelmingly out number the Luftwaffe. After all, there is "safety in numbers" in an air war, too. In addition, the British calculated that losses from daytime bombing would just be too high. Under cover of darkness British bombers would become more difficult targets for German anti-aircraft guns and fighters.

This then became the plan: bomb at night and in overwhelming numbers. To test this strategy Harris decided to unleash an armada of over 1000 bombers on the German industrial city of Cologne. Amidst much politicking and infighting, he convinced the high command that his losses would be low enough, and the devastation of Cologne would be high enough, that it was worth the risk. On the night of May 30, 1942, this great air armada assembled in a stream of bombers some seventy miles long and headed for Germany. They arrived on target near 1:00 a.m. and were met with fierce anti-aircraft fire, but only a few "confused" fighters. As expected, the German air defenses were overwhelmed. Mankind had never seen such a show of force before and the results were totally devastating. Six hundred acres of Cologne were ruined and the British loses were less than 4% of their planes. The new tactic worked. Harris was knighted. Sir "Bomber" Harris now had a plan that he felt would win the war.

Within a few weeks Harris mounted similar raids on Essen and Bremen but the weather didn't cooperate, landmarks were missed, and the remarkable success he achieved at Cologne was not to be repeated. His armada of planes became hard to assemble as those on loan from submarine patrols, training units, and other various outfits began to return to the previous commands from which they had been borrowed for Harris' great experiment. It began to look as if this British strategy of massive nighttime raids might need some additional "tweaking."

Earlier in the year the Big Brass of what was to become the American Eighth Air Force had arrived in England to lay the foundation for the arrival of planes and crews that following summer. They kept an eye on the British strategy, exchanged ideas, and warmly accepted the cooperation and hospitality showed them by their British counterparts. The Americans were led by Brigadier General Ira C. Eaker, who was firmly convinced that *his* boys could successfully carry out strategic daylight bombing even if the British couldn't. Surely eyebrows were raised in the British officers' clubs concerning this brash American approach to the air war, but Eaker was convinced!

The Americans had now begun to produce the Norden bombsight. It was said that a well-trained American bombardier using his Norden bombsight could drop a bomb in a pickle barrel from 4 miles high. And he could! He could at least in the ideal conditions of the clear skies of Arizona, with no flak in the air, and no Messerschmitts on his tail trying to kill him and his crewmembers.

Needless to say, the British were skeptical. On one hand, they were jubilant to have the Americans join them in the air war, for this would further stress the German air defenses, but on the other hand just who did these Americans think they were? The British are a reserved lot, a "stiff upper lip," and all that. In 1942 they were even far more reserved than they are today. This American arrogance, this American bravado, this American cheekiness, was just a bit over the top. Then, to top it off, the Americans began to show up in overwhelming numbers with their garish, gaudy, totally tasteless airplane art. The British thought it bold to decorate their plane with an "I" for Ian, or an "E" for Edward. Descending upon them now were these American planes covered with half naked (or entirely naked) girls, and names like *Impatient Virgin, Piccadilly Commando*, and *Ritzy Blitz*. It was a bit much. The attitude, the nose art, the tasteless names, all added to the famous saying that the trouble with the Yanks is that they are "over-paid, oversexed, and over here!"

The overall commander of the Army Air Corps, "Hap" (for Happy) Arnold, was not only convinced that his American crews and planes could successfully daylight bomb Germany but that the British had simply screwed things up when they made the attempt. His bombsight was better, his tactics were better, his planes were better (the newer model B-17F was becoming available and it had more defensive firepower than earlier models), and he probably felt his crews were better. He could do it. He would do it.

"Bomber" Harris was not at all pleased. It was his opinion that if the American resources were added to his, then the nighttime raids he could mount would be such massive raids on German cities that he could dehouse all of Germany and shorten the war by a considerable amount. This daylight strategy of the Americans would simply dilute the forces available to him. He was annoyed.

It must be remembered that in early 1942 the Americans had not been at war at all, other than the disaster of Pearl Harbor. It wasn't until April of 1942 that Doolittle had raided Tokyo. That first real offensive action by the Americans had done wonders for morale but it had no significant military value. All the while the British had been in the thick of it, beginning in 1939. They had been through Dunkirk, The Battle of Britain, and the campaign in North Africa was underway. They were tough, experienced, veteran soldiers and were none too pleased by these inexperienced "know it alls" from America coming to their shores and telling them how they would run an air war. For their part the Americans had no intention of becoming junior partners. The American way was to play for the varsity, not the junior varsity.

For all of their differences the British were extremely

helpful in preparing the Americans for their new role in this air war. They offered them airfields and helped in training. They helped build storage facilities and barracks. They may have been annoyed, but they were good hosts.

By August of 1942 the Americans felt they were ready to join the fray. On August 17, 1942, the first American daylight precision bombing raid was made to the rail yards of Rouen, France. In the lead plane, in the co-pilot's seat, was Major Paul Tibbets, who would gain fame as the pilot of the *Enola Gay*, the B-29 that dropped the atomic bomb on Hiroshima that essentially ended the war three years later.

This first American attack was limited in size. It consisted of only twelve planes and 160 airmen. (By 1945 the aerial armada would have over 2,500 planes and 25,000 airmen.) The American Air War had begun but clearly more planes and crews would be needed.

On the very day those first American bombs were dropped, the eighteen-year-old Clem Pine was at Jefferson Barracks, Missouri, and about to become an aerial gunner.

As 1942 wound down, the American participation in the air war ramped up. There were raids to Belgium, France, and Holland. Numbers of planes and airmen increased. Tactics changed. Colonel Curtis LeMay, commander of the 305th Bombardment Group decided that the concept of a "stream" of B-17s didn't make the best use of their array of guns and the crossfire they could produce, so he devised a formation known as the "combat box." Essentially it staggered groups of planes both vertically and horizontally so that they could bring maximum firepower on any attacking planes. It demanded close formation flying and 100% attention by the pilot, but LeMay wasn't one to shrink from making demands of his men. The tactic worked and fewer planes were lost.

To no one's surprise these new tactics caused a change in Luftwaffe tactics as well. Up until now the standard attack from the Germans was to approach from behind the last plane or "Tail End Charlie" as it was often called, and try to shoot down the big bombers from the rear. LeMay's Combat Box changed all that and by November of 1942 the Germans had switched their tactics to the frontal assault. It took nerves of steel as the closing speed could exceed 600 mph but it was safer for the German pilots and it put the American pilots, co-pilots and bombardiers at greater risk. The tactics worked. That is, they worked until the newer forts were outfitted with more nose guns, which caused everybody to again rethink their tactics. Such is the way of war.

LeMay's other tactical improvement had to do with bombing accuracy. Each bombardier in each plane had the same Norden bombsight, and often the same target. But bombardiers, like all other people, have varying skill levels from good to bad. Too many bombs were missing their targets. It would be more effective if all the bombardiers were as good as the best bombardier in the flight. LeMay's concept was to put his best man in the lead plane and when he lined up the target in his bombsight he would release his bombs as usual. However, when those bombs were dropped, all the other planes in that combat box would release their bombs at that moment as well. The bombers were not far apart so the bombs ought to land not far apart. It worked, and bombing accuracy improved.

All of these changes, improvements and refinements went on during the end of 1942 but not one American bomb had yet to fall on Germany. The jury was still out. American daylight precision bombing had yet to prove itself as the most effective method to destroy the Third Reich. In fact, Winston Churchill was dead set against this American strategy and was about to veto it altogether when he went to a conference in Morocco in January of 1943. Hap Arnold, fearing this veto, summoned General Eaker to make his best pitch to the Prime Minister and try and convince him of the effectiveness of the American strategy. In the end it all came down to one line, one argument that resonated with Churchill. Eaker argued that with the Americans bombing all day and the British bombing all night, that "By bombing the devils around the clock, we can prevent the German defenses from getting any rest." It made sense to Churchill. He recalled how weary everyone became during "The Blitz," and gave the Americans the OK to proceed.

On the day Winston Churchill gave the thumbs up to the daylight campaign, Clem Pine was flying practice-bombing runs in the deserts of Oregon.

Within a week the first American raid on German soil was organized. The target was Wilhelmshaven, a large naval base on the North Sea. At this point in the war the allies had given submarine destruction the highest priority. Wilhemshaven became such a vital target that it would be bombed nine times before the war ended. (It would be this vital submarine center that would become the target for Clem Pine and his crew on their very first mission nearly five months later.) Of the 53 bombers that reached their Wilhemshaven target that first day, three were shot down. A loss rate of 5% was considered the maximum acceptable in 1943 so, although there was elation at finally hitting Germany, it was somewhat tempered by a loss rate slightly higher than acceptable. Things did not get better. As 1943 unfolded daylight bombing missions by the Americans accelerated. By March, General Eaker had only about 100 bombers ready to fly on any given day. With a loss rate hovering around 5% it wouldn't take long for his strength to be chipped away to the point of ineffectiveness. Eaker launched a paper blitz on Washington that equaled his bombing blitz of Germany. The result was that many planes destined to the Pacific, Africa, or the other theaters of war were being diverted to England.

One of those planes was the *Impatient Virgin* with Clem Pine and his crew aboard.

When the *Virgin* had been stranded for repairs in Marrakech she had been on the way to Oran, Algeria. Clem and his crew had been issued khakis and desert uniforms. Now, due to Eaker's paper pressure on Washington, and the need for crews for the Eighth Air Force, the *Virgin* and her crew luckily drew the assignment that they had all been hoping for all along. England!

CHAPTER 4
THE ROUND TRIP GOES OFF TO WAR

Their first assignment in England was to deliver their *Virgin* to Blackpool, where she would be outfitted for combat, and then returned to them.

You just can't trust the Army.

They turned over their *Impatient Virgin* to the staff at Blackpool as a young couple might leave their newborn with a babysitter for the first time. They never saw her again. Perhaps she got caught up in too much paperwork or army regulations. Maybe there was a sudden need for the plane elsewhere, or maybe there never was any intent to reunite the crew with their plane. There was talk she was sent to Ireland to be refitted with nose machine guns. Whatever the reason, they only saw their beautiful plane again in pictures, posters, and nose art photos.

The crew was assigned to Bovington, England where they were separated by rank and immersed in further training. For Clem, things suddenly turned serious.

In the States everyone had been serious about their training but the real war was still a world away. It existed in newsreels, headlines, and magazines. At Bovington the instructors were honest-to-God veterans! They may have only been twenty years old but last month they had tangled with the Luftwaffe no more than an hour's flight from here. This was *real*! These guys were sharing little tips that damned well might save your life. No more theory here, this was hands-on instruction concerning what to do when your oxygen system froze up solid or your gun jammed. Everybody paid attention. In his two weeks at Bovington, Clem claims to have learned more than he did in all of his stateside classes. Maybe going to war just helps you focus.

Cultural education began to soak in, too. Some of it was in classes concerning those odd British pounds and shillings. Like most of the other kids, this was Clem's first exposure to a foreign country. The beer was warm! They drove on the wrong side of the road! That accent took some getting used to, so did the lasses. There were dances in town and the excitement of London. It was an eye-opening, heart-pounding time of life filled with the exoticness of a foreign land and foreign ways. It was a time of concern, apprehension, and the tension that going to war brings. It was a time of his life that Clem Pine would never forget.

By mid May Clem and his crew were reassembled at Polebrook England to join the newly formed 351st bomb group. During training two of the very best crews had a mid-air collision, killing all on board. Consequently, before the 351st bomb group ever flew a mission they needed two replacement crews to fill out the group. Clem's crew was one of those crews.

First of all they were assigned a new airplane. This time they were denied the opportunity to place their own name on the plane as a previous crew had already had the honor. When 19-

year-old Clem and his hormone-filled crew were still in the safety of America, and about to embark on this grand adventure, they thought the name *Impatient Virgin* would be a pretty cool moniker. The previous crew that had named this new plane probably had cooler, more practical thoughts. Their dreams were not concerned with sexual escapades but with their very survival. At the beginning of May of 1943 the army air corps only expected each plane to last for an average of 11 missions before it was either shot down or too shot up to be air worthy. No crew had yet survived the 25 missions required that would earn them a rotation back to the States. Yes, that previous crew had very much wanted this big bomber to bring them home safely every day. They certainly didn't want a one-way trip to Germany. They wanted her to take them to their target and bring them safely home every day, so they named her *The Round Trip*. It was a good choice.

Training began immediately. Practice bombing missions were flown over the English countryside. Equipment was checked and rechecked. The crew began to learn the idiosyncrasies of *The Round Trip*. Momentum began to build. Any day now would be the first mission. There was tension in the air.

There also was a bit of flamboyance in the air. Except for these two new crews the 351st had all trained together in California. They had become a close-knit group over the past year and to add to their unit pride they had in their midst a celebrity! Captain Clark Gable was assigned to the 351st as a gunnery officer. They were confident.

There were a couple of "false alarms" when they got ready for their first real mission but for some reason each mission was "scrubbed." Usually that was caused by the weather. Then on the night of June 10, 1943 the crew of *The Round Trip* was notified that they would be awakened at 3 a.m. for another attempt at their first mission. One can only imagine what thoughts, what prayers, ran through the minds of, not only those ten young men that night, but of all the crews that would be off to war at dawn. Loved ones and families, good times and bad times, the shortness of their twenty-some years, their relationship with God, their trust in good luck, hometowns and girl friends, romances and sex, faith in their training and the confidence of youthful inexperience, all must have been simmering into the stew of thoughts, dreams, and memories that they all experienced that night. Some slept. Some didn't. For some this would be the last night they would ever experience. Tomorrow, some would be dead.

At 3 a.m. Clem and his crew were awakened. The emotion for Clem that misty morning was excitement. He dressed and headed for the mess hall. The nervous chatter at breakfast ranged from speculation as to where they would be going, to what the weather was like. There was an air of confidence in the room as the young men all headed off for their general briefing. The 351st briefed everyone together, officers on one side, enlisted men on the other. This morning there were about 240 men. Each and every one was intensely interested in what they were about to be told. Would this be a "milk run" to France with little opposition or would it be one of the heavily defended targets in Germany that the Eighth Air Force was starting to engage?

The briefing officer said a few pleasantries, pulled back the curtain revealing the map of Europe, and announced, "Gentlemen, today your target will be Bremen, Germany. Your alternate target will be the German U-Boat yards of Wilhelmshaven." There were a few murmurs, some quiet wise cracks, and some nervous laughter, but every single man in that room knew this would be no milk run. Bremen would be well defended and if the alternate target was chosen this would be the fifth such attack on Wilhemshaven. Just 21 days ago 77 planes had attacked this naval target with seven being shot down and 24 more damaged. No, this was no milk run.

Clem got up and headed for the armament shop. With his two 50-caliber machine guns in hand he then headed out into the dark and across the tarmac for his date with *The Round Trip*. The ground crew was just finishing up. They had the bomber fueled with nine tons of fuel and loaded with 4000 lbs of bombs. Through the damp night these guys had fine-tuned and re-tuned every piece of machinery on that plane that they could get their hands and wrenches on. She was their baby, too. Her silhouette out there in the dark was ominous. A B-17 is an enormous metallic monster absolutely bristling with machine guns from every orifice on the plane. Other than naval ships, in 1943 it was arguably the most lethal war machine ever built. The German pilots all reported their utmost respect for these Flying Fortresses, and this one was Clem's. He stood there in the damp morning darkness and looked up at her with admiration and trust. He was confident *The Round Trip* would be making a round trip that day.

Clem was dressed like an arctic explorer. It would be minus 40F up there so he had on an electric underwear garment, a flying suit, a heavy leather jacket, and a parachute harness. He had thick gloves, sheep skin boots, and an oxygen mask. He was dressed for war as he swung up into the plane and hauled his guns back to the tail. These were Clem's own personal machine guns. He had them highly polished and took care of them as if his survival depended on them. It did. They each weighed about 20 pounds, so first one, then the other, he swung up into the gun case already in the plane. He took off the back plates and slid his guns right into the waiting framework. He adjusted the flexible chutes for his belts of ammunition and was ready for war.

In the misty east the dawn was just breaking. Crews were hanging about waiting for any members who were still getting their specialized briefings. It was a long, cold, thoughtful wait of about an hour. Finally they all assembled and climbed aboard this highly lethal B-17. At this very moment all over England a total of 248 crews were also mounting up. The early morning quiet affected all 2,480 men uniquely. Each pilot and copilot checked each and every switch, button, handle, dial and gauge. The navigators, bombardiers and engineers rechecked their instruments and all the gunners double-checked those machine guns. Those guns were their ticket home.

The smell of hydraulic fluid was pervasive. It mixed with fumes of fuel and rubber into one of those odors that once you've smelled it, you'll never forget it.

Suddenly, out of the early morning dawn a bright green rocket screamed skyward. It lit the morning with an eerie green glow. Just as clearly as the starter at Indianapolis its message was, "Gentlemen, start your engines." At that predetermined moment, all over England those huge Wright Cyclone nine-cylinder radial engines began to whine, crank, wheeze, cough, and sputter to life. These massive bombers began to vibrate as their four huge engines settled into a smooth hum. Each and every engine was run up to full power as the instruments were checked. Their collective roar could be heard all over the early morning English countryside. It was the sound of nearly 3000 young men going to war. Teacups rattled.

The lead plane slowly rolled out onto the runway and like circus elephants the other 23 planes from the 351st followed. Ambulances and rescue trucks raced to the far end of the runway "just in case." The lumbering beasts were surging at their reins. The motors screamed, the propellers grasped at the air, but the brakes held and the nerves frayed. At last someone in command made the call. This flight was a "go." Another green flare streaked skyward and the beasts began the long, slow rumble down the runway. Each plane had the maximum load of bombs and fuel. They weighed about 25 tons each and were in no hurry to leave mother earth. Those emergency vehicles waiting at the end of the runway really had no function at all, for if one of these heavy behemoths staggered and fell from the sky, the fireball would incinerate everything and everyone. You better have trust in your pilot.

When *The Round Trip's* turn came, the gunners all came forward and assembled in the radio room while Cagle eased that massive bomber out on the tarmac. He was a good pilot and they knew it. Slowly he rolled her into the wind. Gradually he picked up speed as those four huge propellers cut into the thick, damp English air. This massive fortress had to fight for every mile-per-hour it could gain as it rumbled down the tarmac. Cagle coaxed every ounce of power out of her as they rolled down that long runway. Tom Petersen, the co-pilot, read out the air speed as these 25 tons of death and destruction lumbered along. At 100 mph they were nearing the end of the runway. The shrubs and hedgerows were fast approaching as Cagle urged her on. Finally, at 120 mph he slowly lifted her up gently into the morning sky. For the first time in his life, Clem Pine was going off to war.

England has always been a dreary, gray-skied setting. Those foggy, cloudy, misty, rainy skies that cause the British to have that pasty-white skin, cause havoc for pilots flying heavy bombers laden with high explosives. As soon as they are airborne they need to climb up through that gray soup without hitting one of the other bombers trying to climb through the same gray soup. On the morning of June 11, 1943, there were 248 such bombers all at about the same time trying to slowly work their way out of clouds. Unfortunately it wasn't all that unusual to have a mid-air collision. Clem recalls with horror in his voice watching two of these huge bombers have just such a collision. Bad things just happen. But Cagle was good. All of his civilian flying experience was paying off now. At about 2000 feet they broke through into dazzling sunlight and that thick gray soup now turned into fluffy mashed potatoes down below. Next came the aerial ballet of assembly. As individual planes these B-17s, even with all their guns, were highly vulnerable to attack by German fighters. Their strength was in numbers, so they now circled over the coast trying to fit into that combat box that Curtis LeMay had developed. Each pilot had been briefed on where his plane fit into the formation but it wasn't always easy to find just the right spot. Then the formation had to form up with the other bomber groups coming up through the soup from their air bases. It was a maddening, fuel-consuming process, but it had to be done if this mass of 248 planes were to fight off the Luftwaffe as they made their way across Germany.

As this armada turned east, up swarmed their "little friends." The British sent a flight of Spitfires to escort these bombers as far as they could. Unfortunately the Spitfires had a limited fuel supply and as the armada looped out over the North Sea the "Spits" simply waggled a "goodbye" with their wings and turned for home. Clem was now all alone in the tail with his twin machine guns. He had test fired them to make sure they hadn't frozen up. He had checked in with Feldstein, the bombardier, who made regular checks just to make sure everyone was OK. He was alert. He scanned the skies continually for German fighters but all he could see was the seemingly invincible mass of 248 B-17s droning along in that starkly blue, clear, rarified air at 25,000 feet. As they turned south and approached Germany it was obvious Bremen was socked in by clouds, so Wilhelmshaven became the target. As they approached the Wilhemshaven naval yards someone up front shouted over the intercom, "Here they come, fighters at twelve o'clock." Sure enough, the Germans had sent about 150 fighters to defend the submarine base. The first bombers they attacked were the lowest ones on the bottom of the formation. This was their usual tactic as they hoped to break up the formation, but the pilots held their positions so that if any of the Germans were brave enough to dive right into the formation they would have to face most of the 2,500 machine guns with which the armada was armed. And they did. It wasn't long before a Messerschmitt made a frontal attack on *Round Trip*. Petersen the co-pilot screamed at Cartwright the top turret gunner, "Get him Cartwright, get him!" as this gutsy German pilot barrel rolled right through the formation. As he went screaming away Clem let loose a barrage with his machine guns, he never knew if he hit him or not, but he knew what it felt like to be at war. "It was so exciting," Clem reports. One can only imagine just how incredibly exciting it must have been for an 18 year old kid all alone in the tail of that massive bomber. By now Messerschmitts and Focke-Wulfs were slicing every which way through the formation. A series of Focke-Wulfs lined up behind Clem's tail and one by one they peeled off and took their turn charging into the formation. As they approached, Clem could see that deadly winking on their wings, which meant that they were lobbing 20-mm cannon shells at the American bombers. Clem waited for each plane to get within about 600 yards and then it was his turn to let loose with his own guns. With his heart thundering, and the adrenaline surging through his veins, Clem sent a burst of machine gun fire at each fighter as it dove into the formation. It clearly was the most exciting moment of his young life. "It was just as exciting as hell," Clem continues to report, with a twinkle in his eye to this day. Gunners everywhere were firing all over the sky. One of the great dangers in such a melee is that with all these teenage kids blasting away with their machine guns, they just might hit one of their own planes. And then it happened. Two 50-caliber slugs from another Fort slammed though the navigator's compartment. One shell tore up all of Dunn's maps and smashed into the radio compass. The other ripped through his pants and left him breathing heavily. When it was all over he discovered a sliver of steel lodged in one of his fingers. Cartwright, in his turret, had also had a close call as he had his headphone cord shot off. Everyone else in the *The Round Trip* was unhurt. For taking that sliver in his bloody finger, Dunn was awarded the Purple Heart. Needless to say, it became the source of a lot of good-natured kidding and joking.

Not every plane was so lucky. As one of the Focke-Wulfs dove into the bomber formation it was hit by machine gun fire. Maybe the pilot was killed. Maybe he just lost control of his plane, but whatever the cause, he went sailing through the bombers and slammed into one of these bomb-laden Fortresses. The explosion was enormous and 11 young men perished in a fiery instant. Other battles were taking place above Clem, below Clem, and all over the sky. It was quite a spectacular show and when it was over eight of these giant bombers and their 80 crewmembers did not make the round trip.

Clem's crew fought their way to the target, managed to avoid being hit by flak and dropped their bombs. They turned for home, met little further resistance, and safely returned to Polebrook.

Mission #1 was complete.

Upon completing the mission each crew was debriefed by an intelligence officer. He wanted to know all the details. How many fighters, of what kind, from what squadrons, were encountered? Were any fighters shot down? Did it appear that the bombs hit the target? Did you see any of our bombers go down and, if so, how many parachutes did you count? It was a thorough session and coffee, hot chocolate, and those yummy Spam sandwiches were offered to the crew. A shot of whiskey was offered, too, as often nerves were shot up as well as airplanes. Clem reports no serious case of nerves. In fact, he claims all the members of his crew stayed ever-confident, calm, and held up well even when under heavy attacks. There was one exception, Dunn the navigator. Dunn was clearly the most nervous guy on the plane. Clem's theory is that being up front, the navigator could see everything that was coming at them. When they were about to fly into heavy flak, he could see it coming. When there was a frontal attack from the Germans, not only could he see it coming, but also he must have felt awfully vulnerable up in that Plexiglas nose. Perhaps one other factor should be remembered. It was Dunn who on that very first mission had a huge bullet pass right through his pants without hitting his leg. Had it struck him it certainly could have taken his leg off and possibly killed him. Sometimes you have a right to be nervous.

Back at the barracks, even though they were exhausted, things turned to pandemonium. All the pent up excitement erupted. "Did you see those two fighters roll right by us?" "How about that one in flames?" "What about those two that criss-crossed right above us?" On and on it went. The excitement of a bunch of teenagers who had just experienced air combat was just indescribable. And it helped that nobody they knew personally had been shot down.

At 3 a.m. the next morning they were at it again. But now they were "veterans." Somewhere out over the English Channel Cagle came on the intercom and told the crew that they were losing engine number two. That meant they had to abort the mission and return to Polebrook. This was not good news. It was these stragglers, or planes that were all alone, that the Luftwaffe was especially eager to find. A single Fort was usually dead meat if it was all alone. It's not at all unlike lions on the plains of Africa singling out a weak animal and they all gang up and attack. *The Round Trip* had become a weak animal. Cagle instantly took her down on the deck. Clem says they were "Suckin' up waves," as they skimmed home over the ocean. The "take her down on the deck" move had become standard operating procedure by mid 1943. The theory was that by flying low, the bombers could not be picked up on German radar and this also took away the Germans' ability to dive down in the attack mode. Flying close to the ground meant a plane attacking you at 400+ mph had to pull up before it could get into ideal shooting range. Clem explains that if the Germans had to attack you from the flat they "leveled the playing field." Fortunately for the crew of *The Round Trip* they made it home without incident and had no need to test this theory.

At 3 a.m. the very next morning they were at it yet again. This time the target was again Bremen. Bremen housed a major Focke-Wulf factory and at this point in the war it was determined that submarine bases and aircraft factories were two of the highest priorities for these heavy bombers. Again there were over 200 bombers on the mission. As they approached the coast of Germany, again that balky number two engine began to lose power. There was already concern aboard, when suddenly the number four engine broke out in fire. This was serious! Over Germany, at 25,000 feet with a flaming engine, and another losing power, they knew they were in for trouble. Cagle instantly took them down to 15,000 feet to relieve them of their need for oxygen. By the time they reached this lower altitude they managed to extinguish the fire but they were still a long way from the safety of England. As they crossed a small German island in the North Sea they dropped their bombs to lighten the load, then it was a race for home. Someone else had just been shot down as they saw a crew in life rafts send up signal flares. They radioed the position to air-sea rescue and headed west. This was not a place to be caught all alone, but for the second day in a row, in their crippled bird, they skated home without encountering any German fighters. It's good to be lucky.

As the afternoon wore on the other bomber crews began to return home. However, for the first time in the war, a crew that Clem knew well did not return. It was the crew commanded by Lieutenant Forest. Forest was a good-looking guy who had quite a swagger about him. He was so good looking in fact that he had no trouble at all with the ladies. It was rumored that when Bob Hope showed up to do his USO show and brought along a bevy of beauties, that Lt. Forest was "successful" with the dames. But tonight in the Bachelor Officer's Quarters there was an empty bunk where Lt. Forest had slept last night. That bothered Clem. As the supply guys came through the barracks to empty out ten beds, ten lockers, ten collections of personal items, it shot the stark reality of the war to Clem and his crew. Those empty bunks were an ugly reminder of what they were up against.

They were credited with another mission but still had 23 left to go.

On their third mission they were sent to France. No fighters were encountered but the crew was gaining in confidence, teamwork and camaraderie. These ten guys were learning to trust each other no matter what the Germans threw at them.

On their fifth mission, the boys were off to France again to bomb an airplane repair facility. Things went smoothly as they crossed the channel and made their way over France. About 20 miles inland all hell broke loose as they were jumped by about 100 German fighters. They managed to fight them off and bomb the target but on the way home they again encountered the Germans that attacked with a renewed vengeance. Crewmembers kept shouting out locations. "Twelve o'clock low, nine O'clock high" and so on, there were planes everywhere. Someone yelled, "Seven o'clock high," and Clem looked up to see a pair of Focke-Wulfs boring in on him. Their wings began winking as they alternated taking shots at *The Round Trip*. Clem estimated the distance he needed to lead the fast charging planes as they closed in and he let loose a stream of machine gun fire. The first plane burst into flames and was gone. He kept firing at the second as it dove on by and under the plane. Clem couldn't tell if he hit it or not but Lodge, in the ball turret, shouted, "You got him, you got him!" as this second plane spiraled out of the sky. When the melee was over two of the other gunners had each shot down a plane, too. So *The Round Trip* had drawn its first blood in its battle over the skies of Europe.

When they returned to their base, they were an excited lot being credited with four German fighters. Clem felt pretty good about it, as did the rest of the crew. He slept well that night. Like all the crewmembers he was well respected, but there was an extra bit of pride as he slept that night. Clem was a good sleeper.

He says he never dreamed of combat or had the night sweats or nightmares that some guys had. In fact, he was such a good sleeper he would sometimes nod off on their long flights into Germany. They would have ten-minute radio checks and when he wouldn't respond they would holler for him to wake up. Petersen claimed, "You're the only bastard I ever saw that could go to sleep on the way to the target."

As the war moved on, so did the strategic thinking inside of allied high command. At first, the top-priority targets had been the German aircraft factories, railway yards and the synthetic oil-producing facilities in Germany. While Harris pursued his dehousing strategy, others felt the priorities should be more toward the German's submarine effort. Coastal command could see that these heavy long-range bombers were just the ticket for long-range Atlantic anti-submarine patrols. The U-boats had crippled allied efforts to ship goods to England and any disruption of their activities would certainly benefit the American shipping effort. Harris felt that was a waste of perfectly good bombers that he could use to cripple the German homeland. It would have been a fascinating exercise to sit inside these decision-making meetings and see how the various branches of the military, the various nations with their own self interests, and each commander with his own big ego and personal priorities bullied, bluffed, negotiated, and finally determined the priority use of these terribly destructive bombers.

By mid 1943, it was determined that if the ball-bearing industry could be wiped out, it would cripple all German war production as those little steel balls were so important to the machinery of war. The list of priorities was endless, constantly evolving, and had to be weighed against practical realities such as each target's distance from England, the weather, current intelligence information, etc.

While Clem Pine and his crew certainly had no say as to what the targeting priorities should be, their lives and fate hung in those targeting decisions that were determined by the high command.

By their sixth mission Clem and his crew were once again caught up in the effort to destroy German submarines and their bases. Once Germany had captured France they set about building submarine bases at the French Atlantic ports. These bases allowed their wolfpacks to easily roam the Atlantic and cause devastating disruption to the allied shipping effort. Clearly the allies had blundered in setting their targeting priorities concerning these bases, because by the time they decided to seriously attack them, the Germans had fortified their facilities with so much concrete that even the one-ton bombs dropped on them simply bounced off. Most of these reinforced structures were a minimum of 12 feet thick and some were well over 20 feet. Nevertheless, on June 28, 1943, Clem and his crew along with 157 other B-17s were sent to destroy the big German naval installation that had been built in St. Nazaire, France. This was a good news/bad news mission for, although it was a relatively short trip to the French coast and back, it was well known that the St. Nazaire submarine base was heavily defended and it just might ignite an engagement with the dreaded "Abbeville Kids." Officially known as *Jagdgeschwader 26*, this elite group of experienced pilots was Goering's pride and joy. They were based at Abbeville, in northwestern France, where they could intercept bomber flights to either Southern Germany or France. They painted their plane's noses a distinctive yellow and this dreaded unit of yellow-nosed fighters developed a nasty reputation among American airmen that was richly deserved.

As the formation of bombers approached the naval base all hell broke loose. First they were swarmed by 180 German fighters. They tried to fight them off but four of the big bombers were shot from the sky. The Germans had not only fortified everything with concrete but they had surrounded their base with a huge array of anti-aircraft guns. Flak began bursting everywhere. Not only could Clem see hundreds of these ominous black puffs all around him but sometimes they burst so close that he could see the red flash of the explosion itself. It was as if they were flying through hell. From their IP (initial point) on, they couldn't deviate on their bomb run; they just had to trust their luck that none of those flak bursts would find them. They were carrying two enormous one-ton bombs that hopefully were powerful enough to blast through all that concrete (they weren't) down below. Over the target it was "bombs away" or at least it was supposed to be. What it was, was "bomb away" because only one bomb had dropped. The other had disengaged from its rack in front, fallen against the bomb bay door and decided to wedge itself half in and half out of the airplane, still hanging by the rear rack. The nose of the bomb was out in the slipstream of the aircraft with its fuse spinning freely. What this did was to arm the bomb as it dangled out of the airplane! Any bump or jolt could set the thing off. As Clem and his nine friends turned for home they were as close to death as any of them had ever been. This was their first real crisis of the war. Something must be done! They had to drop out of formation as this bomb would not only blow up *The Round Trip* if it detonated but it would probably blow several other planes out of the sky as well. Again this made them "sitting ducks" but their only course was to again drop down on the deck and head for home.

Cagle was a take-charge guy. He knew they were in deep trouble and decided he would tackle the problem himself. He left Petersen, the co-pilot, at the controls and climbed back into the bomb bay to survey the crisis for himself. Feldstein, the bombardier, joined him and the two set about trying to delicately disengage the rear bomb shackle that was holding things up. To complicate matters they knew they were flying through the territory of the Abbeville Kids and they couldn't go as low as they would like because when that huge bomb hit the water its explosion would take them with it if they were too low. It was a moment of high drama. Cagle and Feldstein began to pry at the shackle as Petersen aimed them for England. Seven sets of eyes were scanning the skies, as everyone was aware of their ultra vulnerability at this moment. Seconds seemed like hours. They felt very alone when suddenly the bomb released, fell a few hundred feet and set off a massive explosion with a towering geyser right in front of Clem Pine's tail end seat. Perhaps that explosion drew the attention of the Abbeville Kids. Perhaps they had been ready to pounce all along, but as Cagle climbed back into the pilot's seat and dropped them right down on the water the attack began. Fortunately the "on the deck" strategy was working. The two yellow noses couldn't make the classic diving attack or they would have slammed into the sea. Instead, they dropped in behind *The Round Trip*, leveled off (making themselves a much easier target) and as they approached from the rear they began blasting away with their guns. Clem could see from their winking wings that his plane was under attack and as their range closed he lined up his own guns and began to return fire. He never saw his tracers hit the plane; he has no idea if he hit the propeller, the engine, or the pilot, but all at once the dreaded yellow nose that he was shooting at was just gone! It was cart wheeling the short distance into the ocean and with a mighty explosion it simply disintegrated. Clem Pine realized he had just shot down one of the fabled Abbeville Kids. He also had probably saved the lives of his entire crew as the shock of his cart wheeling wing-man had caused the second plane to suddenly go find a safer piece of sky. Nevertheless, in their brief engagement these two German pilots had managed to hit the number four engine of *The Round Trip* and it was now in flames and had to be feathered

This was a bad day.

They had no altitude to work with, they were all alone, their plane was badly shot up, they had an engine on fire, and now they discovered that they were also running out of gas.

This was a real bad day.

Possibly they would have to ditch in the English Channel. Possibly they would be ordered to lighten the plane by throwing out everything they could get their hands on. For Clem in that tail it meant he would have to throw out his machine guns, which was something he *really* didn't want to do. All ten crewmembers began to mentally go through the ditching drill as they crossed their fingers, said their prayers, and hoped for a little luck. They also trusted in Cagle. He was a first-class pilot and knew how to extract every mile possible from a gallon of fuel. He babied that plane along until England was in sight and, as the first possible place to set her down was Bristol, he nursed them onto the ground and ten huge sighs of relief could be heard coming from *The Round Trip*.

Years later Clem modestly says, "It was a real exciting day." It certainly was. What Clem probably didn't realize at the time was what a huge contribution to winning the war he had made that day. When the war ended in both the Pacific and European theaters the enemy had huge numbers of airplanes. To gain air superiority we had tried in vain to bomb their airplane production facilities but it just hadn't been successful. The Germans were masters at dispersing their production facilities and finding hidden places to assemble new planes. We had, however, gained air superiority by the end of the war in both theaters. What had happened was that both the Germans and Japanese were not only running out of fuel by the end of the war but they also had simply run out of experienced pilots. The only planes they could put up by the end of the war were piloted by young kids with very little training. The allied pilots, who by then had vast experience in combat, easily shot them down. It was quite simply a real miss-match.

That yellow-nose Clem shot down on June 28, 1943 was one of Germany's elite few. The pilot would not be replaced by an equal. It was a real loss to Germany and as those Abbeville Kids and other fine pilots went down, the air war began to turn in our favor. The war was not won only by the atomic attack on Japan or on the beaches of Normandy. It was won by thousands of young men like Clem Pine slowly chipping away at the strength of our enemies. Yes, Clem Pine won an important piece of World War II that day in June of 1943.

Every few days through early July, Clem and his crew were scrambled from their early morning beds and sent back over Germany. They even participated in a seven-and-a-half-hour mission to bomb industrial plants in Norway. No two days were the same and it was not always the serious business of war. Most of the guys had acquired bicycles and on days between missions they would ride in to town, go to dances, or have a softball game. The latter always seemed to involve a game against either the Canadians or sometimes the enlisted men would play the officers. On one fine summer day they were having a spirited game against the officers and Clem was doing the pitching. Off in the distance the roar of a motorcycle could be heard as someone came streaking across the base to join the game. It certainly wasn't an enlisted man, as they all rode bicycles. It probably wasn't even an officer unless he was someone very important. So they all stopped and watched, and in a cloud of dust, who should appear but Captain Gable. He hopped off his motorcycle and wanted to join the game. Yes indeed, it was Clark Gable himself. When the war broke out he had signed up and was assigned to the 351st. He trained with them as a gunnery officer in Blyth, California, and was fully determined to do his part in the war effort. Some patriotic movie stars stayed in Hollywood and just made movies about winning the war. Clark Gable actually helped win the war. The Eighth Air Force realized the propaganda disaster they would have if he was killed or captured so they trained him as a gunner and assigned him to fly five very real combat missions while a film crew recorded his every action. They then produced war bond films and some other short patriotic movies to support the morale of folks back in the States. He had a handpicked crew of handsome, photogenic guys, and that motorcycle, but basically Clem reports he was just one of the guys and quite popular. But could he hit? That really was the question as pitcher Clem Pine stared down the movie star. The thought of actually striking out Clark Gable had his head spinning. The thought occurred to others as well and Clem had a bit of a dust up with Connolly who suddenly felt it was his turn to pitch. No Sireee! Clem held his ground, defended his mound, and commenced with his fastball. This was his moment of glory, his fifteen minutes of fame, for when it was over Mighty Casey had been struck out! With a mile-wide grin, Clem today says that his claim to fame in this life was that he struck out Clark Gable in a softball game and in later years he beat Chuck Yeager in a skeet-shooting match!

But after a day of softball glory it was back to the war. After completing ten missions, the crew of *The Round Trip* was about to participate in one of the most profound events of World War II.

The British had been developing a system of dropping millions of strips of aluminum foil to confuse the German radar. They were now ready to use it in conjunction with Sir "Bomber" Harris' concept of dehousing the German population. The target, soon to be the victim, of this strategy was Hamburg. Hamburg was an important industrial center and its position on the Elbe River made it an easy target to locate. On the night of July 24, 1943, The British RAF sent 740 bombers over Hamburg. They released 92 million aluminum strips, which appeared on German radar as thousands of planes. It utterly confused the defenders and the RAF then rained 3,000 tons of bombs on the sleeping city. The results were devastating. The dehousing program had just begun.

As these RAF bombers returned home from their nighttime assault on Hamburg, Clem and his crew were being rousted out of bed for a daylight attack on the same city. The "bomb the devils 'round the clock so they can't get any rest" campaign was underway. *The Round Trip* plus 67 other B-17s made their way into Germany only to be greeted by a host of angry German pilots doing their best to protect Hamburg. The defense they put up was spectacular. They tangled with the big American planes as they approached Hamburg, as they left Hamburg, and all the way out of Germany. According to Sergeant Cartwright, the engineer on Clem's crew, "Several B-17s and a mess of fighters went down." Due to poor visibility, *The Round Trip* had to dump her bombs on the city of Nordenham. But the visibility over Hamburg had been good enough for Clem to see the utter devastation wrought by 780 British planes the night before.

Hamburg was a city in flames but her troubles were far from over. She was being dehoused with great success. The following day the Americans returned again to bomb the power plants of Hamburg. The city was left to recover and fight its massive fires for only a day before "Bomber" Harris was back at work with his nighttime armada of 722 planes. As the British planes approached the city that night they could see the flaming inferno below for miles and miles. Their previous raid plus the two American daylight attacks had ruined Hamburg's fire fighting defenses. Water lines had burst, bridges were down, and rubble blocked the streets. The city lay helpless that night beneath this massive bomber force that poured its load of destruction into the flaming city. The result of these additional tons of bombs created what may have been the worst fire in mankind's history. *Everything* in Hamburg was burning. Homes, trees, vehicles, asphalt, animals, people, were all being incinerated as temperatures reached 1800 F. This incredible heat began to rise into the sky. As it did so, the cooler air surrounding Hamburg rushed in toward the center of the city to replace the superheated air that was rising skyward. This wind blowing into the city from all sides simply fanned the flames and the fire became greater and greater, sucking in air from all sides at up to 150 mph. That's the wind speed of a category-5 hurricane. These howling winds blowing into Hamburg were now not only furnishing the fire with oxygen but with fuel as well. Winds of 150 mph rip trees right out of the ground. They will pick up anything and everything in their path and sweep it into the fire, including human beings by the score. This fire had become a storm. Hamburg was the first victim of World War II to suffer the inhumanely awful fate of a firestorm, but it wouldn't be the last.

Unfortunately for Hamburg the bombing went on for nine

days. When it was over nearly ten square miles of Hamburg was quite simply gone and over 50,000 were dead. Sir "Bomber" Harris had mastered the art of dehousing. The events of Hamburg would change the course of the war. It was one of those events that cause side A to again change its strategy.

For the Germans Hamburg became known as *Die Katastrophe*. Albert Speer, the minister for armaments, claimed Hamburg "Put the fear of God in me." He told Hitler that if the allies hit six more industrial cities like they did Hamburg, it would bring Germany to her knees. It was a grave moment for Germany. The result of it all was increased fighter production and the rotation of some of Germany's best pilots from the eastern front back to defend the Fatherland. At one point, fully 65% of Germany's fighter force was devoted to fending off these devastating aerial attacks.

CHAPTER 5
MISSION COMPLETED

As July rolled into August of 1943, Clem and his crew continued to fly missions to Germany and France. Often they met heavy fighter resistance or sometimes it would be just flak. On a mission to Kassel to bomb an aircraft factory a flak shell exploded just outside of the top turret, which housed Sgt. Cartwright the engineer. Part of the exploding shell smashed through his turret, clipped him on the neck as it went past, severed his headphones, hit his gun sight, and sprayed the turret with glass. He was unhurt. Had he been an inch or two to the left he probably would have died. Clearly every mission involved more luck than a dice game. On that very mission, ten Forts did not make it home. A hundred more guys had just rolled craps.

Tourist Pine even had an all-expense paid trip to Paris. On August 16 *The Round Trip* and 170 other bombers headed for Paris to bomb airfields and gasoline dumps. The day was unusually clear. That deep blue sky at 25,000 feet and the crystal clear air that morning made it a sightseer's dream. German fighters appeared but as the bombers were escorted by American P-47s the Germans never got close enough to disrupt the sight seeing. The crews could quite easily make out the

Eiffel Tour, the Arc de Triumph and the various landmarks of that beautiful city. For the crew of the *The Round Trip*, seeing Paris for the first time was not only quite a novelty but also it was their 15th mission. Only ten more and they would be going home.

On the very next day things were to change dramatically.

On August 17, the mission planners unveiled their most ambitious targeting yet. This was to be a "maximum effort." It would entail two separate groups of bombers that were to simultaneously attack both the aircraft factories at Regensburg and the ball bearing factory at Schweinfurt, both of which were in Southeastern Germany. The missions would require flying nearly 3 hours, unescorted over Germany itself, but the theory was that so many bombers would simply overwhelm the number of fighters that the Luftwaffe could put up. Over 360 bombers were scheduled for the mission and the planning called for them all to arrive over Germany at the same time.

Clem and his crew were tired, as they had been to Paris the day before. At 3 o'clock in the morning they were rousted and sent off to breakfast and briefings so they could be prepared for a 5:05 a.m. take off. At the briefing there was an audible gasp as the map was unveiled and they saw their target was Schweinfurt. Never before had the bombers penetrated so far into Germany. This mission was going to put them over Germany for several hours with no fighter protection. To mitigate this danger the plan to overwhelm the German defenses was carefully explained. In addition a thorough case was made as to the importance of these targets. This was the straw that would break Hitler's back. Some of the crews were told that this raid would be so devastating to the Nazi war machine that within three months they would simply "throw in the towel." Clem acknowledges that the hype made them feel that this was the raid that would stop the war.

After the briefing, all of the crewmembers collected their equipment and trudged out to their plane as the sun was about to rise. They went through their pre-flight routine and then sat down to wait for the signal to "mount up." They smoked cigarettes and they waited. They stretched out for a nap and they waited. They wished they had brought a deck of cards and they waited. The sun rose high in the sky and still they waited. It was nearly noon before the signal to mount up was given and they finally took off at 12:05 p.m.

Unbeknownst to Clem and his crew was the fact that the planes destined for Regensburg had lifted off much earlier. As these Regensburg bound bombers crossed the Channel and were soon over Germany they were met by over 300 German fighters that extracted a heavy toll on them. The Schweinfurt raiders were still on the ground and therefore couldn't help dilute the effect of all those German fighters. It also meant that when the Schweinfurt bound planes did finally arrive over Germany that the Nazi's had had time to land, refuel, replenish their ammunition, and send those same 300 planes up against this new wave of bombers.

Never before had the American bombers faced such a variety of weaponry as the Germans unleashed that day. Not only did they have to fly through the withering firepower of the usual machine guns and cannon shells, but also now, the Germans began to shoot time-fused rockets into the formations from quite some distance out. The German planes would stay out of range of the B-17s guns and lob in these rockets that weighed nearly 250 pounds and were set to explode inside the bomber formations. The Germans also flew their own bombers up and above the American formation. They then dropped their own bombs, which were timed to go off as they passed through the American planes. The results were devastating. According to Cartwright, *The Round Trip's* engineer, "They really gave us hell. I saw B-17s go down both in front of us and behind, as many as five at a time. I also saw a fighter explode in mid-air just like a flak shell. The sky was full of parachutes beneath us. Some forts simply fell out of formation end over end. Others would peel out of control and do slow rolls, stall or crash dive. It was terrible to see, especially when we knew it may be our turn next, we succeeded in keeping them off us, but they kept attacking all the way to the target." Clem reports that he could see "those big beautiful birds going down everywhere." One of the planes flying right next to *The Round Trip* simply disintegrated in a massive explosion that pushed *The Round Trip* up through the sky. It was obvious that all ten men aboard had perished in the fireball. One can understand Clem's amazement when after the war he met a crewmember from that plane who had survived! When asked how, he had no explanation for his survival other than he simply awoke floating beneath his parachute. It was an unforgettable day with unbelievable losses. When they finally reached their target they had been over Germany for an hour and a half of non-stop combat.

There had been so much action in the skies that Clem was now devastated as he realized that he was totally out of ammunition. So were some of the other gunners on his plane. It was a time of desperation, as they still had to fly another 90 minutes to reach the relative safety of American fighters. Clem reports he was "damn near in tears." He found it very hard to just sit there and take it, and not be able to defend himself and his plane. He could detect a sense of panic in the voices over the intercom. They all could see that their formation was now in disarray as so many planes had been lost and this disorganization made them highly vulnerable to attack. They did their best to reform into position and every time they were attacked Cagle would put *The Round Trip* through whatever defensive moves he could, but being in even a loose formation his evasive maneuvering was limited. After what seemed like an interminable 90 minutes they finally escaped the German fighters, and after crossing Belgium and the English Channel landed at an auxiliary airfield for fuel. They then limped back to their home field at Polebrook, only to march into a debriefing that Clem describes as "real bad." To put it frankly, he says that everyone was pissed off. They knew that the coordination of the Regensburg/Schweinfurt groups had been fouled up and it had cost lives, a lot of lives. On that terrible day of August 17, 1943, the Eighth Air Force had lost 60 B-17s. That night there were 600 beds empty. There were 600 mothers and fathers to notify that their sons had been lost. Not only was the effect of these losses devastating to the American Air Force, but when the war was over, and the true effect of these air raids could be studied, it was learned that, although the bombing of Regensburg and Schweinfurt had substantially damaged the targets, it had hardly crippled the Germans at all. Until the day the war ended the Germans never ran short of planes or ball bearings.

It was time for Side B to again change its strategy.

On the Regensburg/Schweinfurt raid the Americans had lost more than 15% of their planes. At that rate of loss they would have no planes left after only a week! Something must be done! So the decision was made to wait for the arrival of the new American P-51 Mustang fighters that had such long-range capabilities that they could escort the bombers all the way to Berlin and back if need be. In fact, of the ten missions Clem still had to fly, he would only return to Germany one more time. The rest were to Belgium or France, not that Belgium and France were always "milk runs;" in fact, on his very next mission Clem and his crew were all reported as being killed in action.

The mission was to St. Omer, France. *The Round Trip* was unfortunate enough to be the lowest and last plane in the formation. As they crossed the French coast they really caught hell from the German fighters. Everyone was shooting; there was action everywhere when the B-17 flying next to them simply disintegrated in one massive explosion. Apparently one of the German flak shells had penetrated the plane and set off all their bombs in one catastrophic explosion. The rest of the American planes flying up above were sure it was *The Round Trip* that had exploded and reported it so, as they were the first to return to Polebrook. One can imagine the surprise when the badly shot-up *Round Trip* limped home displaying a huge hole in the vertical stabilizer. But it had made the round trip once more.

On their next mission to France, as soon as they crossed the English Channel two of the bombers up above them collided, and as they spun to earth one of them crashed into a third bomber and all three planes were lost. There was nothing easy or safe about this war. In fact, of all of the large units of the military service the most dangerous during World War II was to be in a bomber crew. Clem said he thought it was a great job, as every night you slept in your nice warm bed. He felt sorry for those GIs down there in their muddy foxholes. He certainly was warmer but he was surely not safer. The average life of a B-17 was just 11 missions. Either it would be shot down or so shot up it couldn't fly again. The expected losses were 5% on each mission. Crews were required to fly 25 missions before being rotated back to the States. That meant the probability of their survival was just 27.7% Anyway you look at it, warm beds or not, those are TERRIBLE odds.

It seemed as if the Eighth Air Force wanted to push those odds a little lower. On September 6, 1943, Clem and the boys were sent on what was to be their last trip over Germany. They were shocked to see the target was the aircraft industry of Stuttgart. It was even farther from home than Schweinfurt! Of the 338 bombers launched, only a very few found their targets as the weather turned so rotten. Everyone else just dumped their bombs on "targets of opportunity." Fortunately the German defenses were not as intense as on the Schweinfurt raid so not as many bombers were shot down. Their problem came with fuel consumption. It was a very long flight and so many planes spent time searching for their targets that they simply ran out of gas on the way home. Twelve bombers had to ditch in the English Channel. Most of the crews were rescued but it certainly drove home the message that there were a lot of ways to get killed in this air war, especially when you only had five missions to go.

Now was the time to get nervous. When the air war began for Clem Pine it was just "exciting as hell," as a 19-year-old kid he felt bullet proof, off on a grand adventure, but now, as his time became short, and there were only a few missions to go, it was time to worry. He was hoping for "milk runs" and although missions 21–24 turned out to be shorter flights into France and Belgium they certainly weren't "milk runs."

On the morning of September 23, 1943, Clem and the boys were rousted for their last mission. Their crew was highly unusual in that they had essentially been together for the first 24 missions. It was common for some crewmembers to get killed, wounded, or just sick and miss some missions, so that when the "last" mission finally arrived, the drama of the event was not shared by all. Only Alex Feldstein, the bombardier, had ever missed a mission. (He would have to fly one more mission with another crew to complete his tour.) The Crew had not only painted a bomb on *The Round Trip* every time they successfully completed a mission, but they also painted another bomb on the back of their prized leather flight jackets. As the missions mounted up, the bombs began to cover the jackets and the status of their owners increased accordingly. Quite frankly, they felt like they were pretty hot stuff! It was an exciting morning for Clem. There were a lot of flyers that morning that knew these boys were heading out on their last mission. As they sauntered off to breakfast they had a little extra swagger in their step. You can walk that way when you're pretty hot stuff!

On September 23, 1943 there were not many crews that had successfully completed 25 missions. With the odds being only 27.7% most crews had simply not survived. The *Memphis Belle* and a few others had indeed done it, but it was still a special morning to be sending *The Round Trip* out on her final mission. The briefing that morning had a little extra tension as the target was indicated as a sub-tender that was anchored in a river just south of heavily defended St. Nazaire, France. They were to have American P-47 Thunderbolts escort them all the way to the target and back, so things looked pretty good.

Takeoff and assembly went as planned but where were the P-47s? They never showed up! Oops. What a day to have such bad coordination! As they approached the initial point to begin their bomb run they could see there was a front over the target so they had to drop down to 15,000 feet. Immediately they were pounced upon by German fighters. The flak was terrific. This was just not how it was supposed to be on your last mission, but miraculously, when all the bombers emerged from the bomb run, none had gone down. Now to get home. They had planned to cross France, but once again were jumped by about 20 fighters and the melee was on. They dropped down to 4000 feet, headed out to sea, and ran for home. Everybody had survived! It now began to sink in to Clem and his crew that they really had survived the war. At times it had seemed impossible but here they were heading for home with a plane full of jubilation. It was time for their big show, their celebration. You were *NEVER* to buzz the airfield, but upon completion of your 25th the unacceptable somehow became an acceptable practice. The elated crew zoomed in over the airfield and flew back and forth several times. They buzzed the runway, the mess hall, the ball field and the barracks. They were showing off and they knew it. And they loved it! They finally landed and taxied up to their assigned spot for the very last time. They were just as ready as could be for all of the cheering flyers, ground crews, and photographers, who would greet them and help them celebrate their remarkable achievement. This was gonna be fun!

They came piling out of their beloved *Round Trip* only to find nobody was there to greet them! What was wrong? Where were all the cheering crowds, maybe even a brass band? What a let down!

As it turned out, at that very moment another bomber had just landed, bringing home an equally jubilant crewmember who had just flown his fifth and last mission. It was none other than Major Clark Gable! Needless to say the photographers and crowds had all gone to see the movie star finish his last assignment. It was a tough moment for Clem. "We were all pumped up like hell for group pictures and congratulation," Clem reports. "We were disappointed, we really were."

Life can be so unfair when you're not a movie star!

One can imagine that Alex Feldstein, the bombardier, must have been a bit envious of his nine crewmembers who had just completed their 25 missions. He still had one more to fly and had to wait 11 more days for a crew to need a substitute bombardier. On October 4th he was excited, as it was his turn for glory, celebration, and the honor of completing his 25th and last mission. Unfortunately, on his last bomb run a piece of flak came hurtling through the aluminum skin of the bomber, hit Feldstein in the head, and he was killed in action.

War.

CHAPTER 6
BECOMING A POW

Being finished with 25 missions did not mean this crew was through with the war. After all, their contribution had taken just a few months, and the war was still raging in September of 1943. Cagle sat down with each crewmember and counseled them as to what they would like to do for their next assignment. Ten guys had ten different ideas. The crew was split up with Clem going to Chettington for three months to become one of those veteran gunners who would teach the rookies the art of aerial warfare. Professor Pine was only 19 but everyone paid close attention as he put them through the "machine gun malfunction" class. Clem felt useful, as he knew full well the life and death importance of what he was teaching. He could feel the riveted attention of each and every student one day when the door was pushed open, and from the rear of the room came the unmistakable accent that every movie fan the world over could recognize. "Are these guys paying attention and learning anything?" questioned Jimmy Stewart. Stewart piloted a B-24 and had entrusted his gunnery crew to the experience of Clem Pine. That lesson must have been well learned as Stewart certainly made it though the war and back to his career in Hollywood.

It was a quick, easy three months and when it was over he found himself on a liberty ship heading home, spending Christmas at sea. Clem had always had good timing and it certainly hadn't left him now, for when he reached New York harbor it was New Year's Eve. The returning fliers stood out on the deck and watched fire works rain down over Lady Liberty herself. It was a New Year's Eve to remember. It was a New Year's Eve that left a lump in the throat. It was good to be home.

When Clem had signed up he knew he was going off to war. Gosh it was exciting. All of that schooling was meaningful; it was important. It meant survival. The bonding of his crew and that grand adventure of those young kids taking *The Impatient Virgin* to South America, then across the Atlantic Ocean to Africa, and on to Europe was an adventure of the highest order. It was all building to a powerful climax. It was dangerous as hell, but my God, it was exciting to be going off to war with the greatest bunch of guys he had ever known.

Now it was over.

Yes, it was good to be home but there was an emptiness about it, especially for a 19-year-old kid. Clem spent time at various bases. He went home to California to see his mother and had a great thirty days at the Edgewater Hotel, which was right on the beach in Santa Monica. He enjoyed the beach life with other returned fliers but that edge that he had known in the tail of his B-17 was gone. And there was a war still going on! D-Day had not yet occurred. There was obviously going to be an invasion in the near future and it sure would be exciting to be a part of it. This was still early 1944 and it was not yet obvious that Germany would be defeated.

Clem was sent to Galveston, Texas, to spend some time as a

has-been warrior. Now it was time to goof off. Now was the time for those meaningless tasks the Army has always been so famous for. Clem spent time loading sand into phony practice bombs. In the afternoons he and his buddies would sneak off to speak-easy type joints and drink beer. Yes, it was fun. Yes, they had some good times, but nothing in the rest of his life would ever compare to those eight months he had just spent in England. Those days over Nazi Germany, crouched in the tail of *The Round Trip*, firing those machine guns, while he and his buddies fought for their very lives would be the defining event of his life.

This new life was just plain dull. Within six weeks Clem had made the decision that he would rather go back to the war than wither away filling sand bombs in Texas.

There are times and places and people and events in life that just can't be repeated. Things just serendipitously fall together sometimes in the most providential of ways. For some it was in high school. Maybe your team won the state championship. For others it was college, or maybe those days at the fraternity house. It might have been your platoon in the army or the guys you went through basic training with. It might have been any set of circumstances and friends that come together for a brief period of life that simply bond good friends and special circumstances into a private world that no one else will ever know or appreciate. What also is for sure is that those times just can't be repeated. Some say, "You can never go home again." Some just refer to them as "the good old days." Whatever the case, whatever they are called, you just can't repeat them.

Clem tried. He signed up for another tour and was sent to Alexandria, Louisiana, and assigned to a new crew. It just wasn't the same. The chemistry of the crew wasn't the same.

Nothing was the same. The war wasn't even the same. By the time Clem and his new crew returned to join the 91st Bomb Group at Bassingbourn, England, in August of 1944, the allies had gained air superiority over Germany. What was left of the Luftwaffe had not even contested D-Day. Day by day those Abbeville kids had been shot down. Week by week those pilots defending the Fatherland had been killed and the green kids who replaced them were just no match for the veteran pilots of the U.S. Air Force who were now flying long-range P-38 Lightnings, P-47 Thunderbolts and P-51 Mustangs that escorted the big bombers all the way to Berlin and back. Yes, the war had changed in the seven months that Clem had been away. As the danger from the Luftwaffe receded, a waist gunner was pulled off of each crew so only 9 guys now made up a team. As the skies were safer it now took 30 missions to complete a tour. When Clem arrived back in England he even talked to guys who had flown 10 or 15 missions and never fired their guns! This time things should be easy.

On his first missions on this second tour Clem realized that things might be different but they were not going to be easy. There were far fewer German fighters to contend with, but now the Germans had established massive flak batteries to defend their cities. On his second mission the flak was so intense that Clem recalls mumbling, "Holy shit. This is crazy! This is pretty stupid coming back here." Even so, Clem recalls feeling like a "passenger" on his first three flights. It was quite a show watching the American fighters, the "little friends," mix it up with the few German fighters who did dare to challenge this huge armada of air power that now was arriving daily over the Fatherland. He never even fired his guns on those first three missions.

Then came mission number four.

Mission number four was different from his other missions in that this time they would not be dropping any bombs. Their payload on this particular day was thousands of propaganda leaflets commonly called "nickels." It was also different for Clem because it was the last mission he would ever fly.

It was August 16, 1944 (the day that this story began), when Clem had that awful feeling that they were flying dangerously close to that layer of clouds above them. They were so close to the clouds that there was no way the little friends could protect them if the Germans were to pounce out of that fluffy white stuff. It was only a matter of 40 seconds from the time that those six beautiful blue Focke-Wulf 190s materialized out of thin air until the time that Clem Pine found himself dangling perilously below his parachute with his leg and wrist badly shot to pieces. No, things were not going to be easy.

Clem had about ten minutes to adjust to his new world. He had gone from a swaggering gunner, who for 25 missions had been part of an elite team of men, to a bored has-been in Texas, to a last-minute addition to an awkwardly assembled crew of nine, to a very wounded, scared kid who was now drifting down into Nazi Germany and about to become a prisoner of war. Clem had never made a parachute jump before. He had some classroom instruction, but that was it. If there ever was "on the job training" Clem Pine was getting it right now! When his chute popped open it delivered an awful jolt to his damaged body. It hurt! He was still in the middle of this air war with the German fighters attacking the B-17s. The bombers were blazing away with over 100 machine guns and six of the flaming bombers were now careening to earth. As he hung there, this raging battle kept moving away from him. He was being totally ignored! They had just left him all alone in his own little piece of the German sky. As he descended he had plenty

A propaganda leaflet or "nickel" similar to the ones Clem Pine's plane was dropping on the day he was shot down.

of time to inventory his damaged body. He had no thoughts of evasion, as he knew his wounds were serious. All he could hope for was to safely land with that bad leg intact and not to be killed by an angry mob as so many fliers had been. Soon everything was silent. The air battle had flown away and he was still five miles above the earth. He had heard stories about how you could pull on the lines and "spill" some air to change your direction of descent, but he was so thankful that his chute had opened and was doing its job properly that he came quickly to the "if it ain't broke, don't fix it" frame of mind. The time to hone your parachuting skills is not on your first jump, while wounded, about to become a POW, over Nazi Germany.

As he dropped ever closer to captivity he could see that he was going to land on a hillside in a forest. As the earth approached he began to hear the shouting voices of people on the ground. They knew he was on his way and they intended to greet him! One of the few things he could remember from parachute class was to cross his legs if he was coming down in a tree. So with legs crossed, knees bent, and his heart in his throat, Clem Pine crashed into Germany. Luck was on his side. Clem recalls that he hit the pine tree as if it was just a big cushion. He missed all the big limbs, bounced around and without so much as a scratch he found himself dangling just a foot or two off the ground. He slipped out of his harness and dropped to the ground on his good leg.

Now what?

Now it was time for pain.

The shock of being shot out of the sky and the parachute ride had masked Clem's pain, but as he lay there in the forest he began to feel serious agony. Considering the fact that his leg was so full of shredded steel (some of it remains there today) it is amazing that it had taken so long for the pain to set in, but by now it had set in, in spades. After a few minutes he could hear a crowd somewhere at the bottom of his hill. They had just seen six B-17s come crashing out of the heavens into their neighborhood and they were on the lookout for airmen. Clem began to call to them and in a few minutes he was surrounded by a mob of not-too-friendly Germans. His major concern was a scowling railroad worker who looked like a junkyard dog. Before he could inflict any damage to Clem, a young teenaged boy who could speak some English began to ask Clem lots of "stupid" questions. "Are you a pilot?" "What city are you bombing?" They were the sorts of questions that this 14-year-old surely didn't care about, but it made him feel like an official interrogator. It just annoyed Clem. Finally, a middle-aged woman, who probably had kids of her own, about Clem's age, asserted herself and removed Clem's dirty scarf from his neck and began to bandage his wounded leg. She produced a roll of crepe paper bandages that were common in Germany in those days, and wrapped his entire leg. Here things get fuzzy. Clem thinks he was drifting into shock at this point as he lost contact with time and place. When he again became fully conscious he was on a stretcher surrounded by five or six other captured American airmen and a couple of German military guards who took them to a recently-bombed train station.

    Now was the time for the angry mob. One can only imagine the furor and hatred fermenting in the civilians in any country who have just had their homes demolished and their families blown to bits. By August of 1944 that daily armada in the skies of these giant bombers must have worn the German civilians to the frazzle point. They were just so defenseless and impotent. There was nothing at all they could do to defend their homes and lives from all this death and destruction raining from the sky. If only they could get their hands on the people who had created all this carnage!

Things got ugly fast.

"*Luft gangster, schweinhund, terrorflieger,*" and assorted other greetings were hurled at these despondent airmen. Country folk began to gather and kept hurling obscenities, gestures and their loathing at the airmen. This venomous crowd continued to grow as people emerged from houses, alleys, and the train station itself. It was obvious they all wanted a piece of the action. They each wanted their own piece of revenge on these gangsters from the sky. Clem was one of two guys on stretchers. The rest of the Americans set them on the ground and then each took a knee. They became as non-threatening as six guys can be but still the mob surged forward. Clem was seriously worrying about his life when that not-to-be-mistaken sound of "kerchunk kerchunk" could be heard as the two guards each jacked a bullet into the chamber of their bolt action rifles. That telltale sound began to subdue the mob. The guards stood tall, asserted their military authority, and six American airmen knew they had just barely escaped being beaten to death by an angry mob.

The train soon arrived and hauled them off to Frankfurt and Dulag Luft. This was a special interrogation center where all captured airmen were grilled for useful information. Expecting to undergo the type of interrogation seen in the movies, Clem was pleasantly surprised to find himself undergoing nothing but a superficial questioning. By now the Germans realized that a group of airmen who had been captured for more than a day had plenty of time to concoct a good story, and besides, this was August of 1944. The allies had broken out of their D-Day beachhead and were swarming across France. Italy was falling. The Russians were advancing from the east. As Clem says, "At this point in the war there were not many mysteries about what these bombers were up to." It was also obvious to his interrogator that Clem was now in a lot of pain so he was simply sent off to the little hospital they maintained for wounded allied flyers.

(To this day Clem Pine says he will be eternally grateful that he was shot down over Europe and not the Pacific. Whereas most prisoners of the Japanese were treated in a horrific manner, the Germans treated him with respect, decency, and their medical staff probably saved his life.)

Now real fear set in. It had been three or four days since that cannon shell had ripped through and imbedded a good part of itself in Clem's leg. Frankly, it was beginning to stink and it hurt like hell. Clem understood clearly that this was all pointing to the probability that he was about to lose his leg. An orderly came in and unwrapped the original bandage and the scarf that was applied when he had landed. As the putrid odor hit the orderly his head snapped back and he went to find a medical book. He returned to show Clem pictures of gangrene, just as Clem had feared.

The idea of losing a leg must be absolutely awful to any human being, but it must be doubly so when you are just 20 years old. By now, Clem could tell that from the way the Germans were treating him that he would survive the war, it was just a matter of time. But the idea of losing that leg to a young man of 20, in the prime of life, was just overwhelming. That evening they carried him off on a stretcher to the room used for operations. A big, blond civilian doctor began to examine his leg as they administered a general anesthetic. Just before he went under, Clem asked the doctor, "Are you going to cut my leg off?" The doctor, who didn't look very positive, slowly shook his head and answered, "I don't know."

Everyone who has gone off to combat has his story of fate.

A shell explodes and one guy is killed and another isn't. Some guys get blown to bits and others don't ever get a scratch. Some lose their legs and some don't. Fate? Destiny? Luck? As Clem slowly awakened and realized where he was his immediate reaction was to feel for his leg or what was left of it. It was still there! The doctor had decided to just clean it out and pack it with Vaseline gauze, bandage the whole thing, and not to stitch it up. But he still had two legs!

Soon Clem was off on the train to Stalag 9C where there was a big hospital for recovering allied soldiers. Amazingly, on his wing of the hospital there were no Germans to be seen. No guards, no doctors, no Germans at all. The floor had about 60 patients and was administered by British "inmates" who filled most of the beds. Clem would spend from late August until the first part of November on that floor and as he retells his stories it is obvious that other than his months with *The Round Trip* crew this was his best wartime experience. Once again a group of young men all facing the same sort of problems, with the same set of concerns, were thrown together and they quickly formed that special bond. They organized cleaning details, they organized their own food, and they took care of each other, both physically and emotionally.

Clem made good friends with Dave, a Canadian medic, who would come by every day and unlace his leg splint. Dave would remove the Vaseline gauze and carefully pick through the wound. It seemed that when Clem came crashing down through that pine tree bits of bark, pine needles, and grit of all sorts, had been wedged into his leg wound. The German doctor had removed most of the material but he hadn't the time to get every little bit, so Dave would take his forceps and pick bits out of Clem's leg as long as he could stand it. When the pain became too much, Dave would re-pack the leg and lace up the splint, only to return the next day to continue his project.

Every few days Dr. Barling, an Australian doctor, would make the rounds to see how everyone was doing. Clem was satisfied with his leg's progress but his wrist wound just kept oozing and wouldn't heal, so he asked the doctor to take a look. Dr. Barling took one look and announced, "Well shit, you still have a piece of shrapnel up in there!" He took out a pair of forceps, rammed them down Clem's arm and yanked out a chunk of steel. It hurt like the devil but in no time at all Clem's wrist finally healed up nicely.

As the autumn progressed this international band of wounded brothers became good friends. Jock, the Scot, even had kilts he would wear on Sundays. If they had received food packages from the Red Cross they would often contribute food and Jock would fix them a big bread pudding. Life wasn't too bad, considering they were all POWs.

By October the medical people determined it was finally time to sew up Clem's long leg wound. In the operating room they placed a long perforated tube the length of the wound and sewed his leg up, around the tube. Then, from time to time, they would bring along this new wonder drug called "penicillin" and pour it into the tube. It was a technique that never became a standard procedure, but it worked! Within a few weeks Clem's leg was healing up nicely even though he still had chunks of shrapnel buried deep in his muscles.

By mid November Clem had been shipped from one recuperation stop to another. He had gone from crutches to limping, and was now able to walk reasonably well. One morning the Germans came through and separated Clem and about a dozen of the healthiest patients from all of the amputees and put these "healthy" guys on a train headed north. Clem didn't know it at the time but he was now on his way to

Pomerania, what is today Northern Poland, and was about to be deposited into Stalag Luft 4, right in the midst of the German POW system.

CHAPTER 7
STALAG LUFT 4

"A" Lager of Stalag Luft 4 as seen from the guard tower.

It's very difficult to research what plans the Germans had for prisoners of war. It's harder yet to get into the heads of Hitler, Himmler, Speer, Goering and the rest, and to know what they were really thinking. The "Final Solution" for the Jewish "problem" is well documented but the upcoming disposition of tens of thousands (and then hundreds of thousands) of allied military men is seldom mentioned. It seems as if so many POWs just weren't expected. The Germans seemed to be planning on a thousand-year Reich so their first assumption must have been that they were going to win the war and conquer the world. The ease of their Blitzkrieg through Poland and the way they ran the allies out of France at Dunkirk must have been very reassuring to the High Command. It certainly looked for a while as if World War II would be a "cake walk" for the German military.

By 1940 Britain looked like an easy next victim. Operation Sea Lion was ready to invade England as soon as those pesky British boys in their Spitfires and Hurricanes could be dispensed with. It seems probable that, had the German invasion of Britain been successful (from the German point of view), the defeated English army would have just withered away as the Polish army had done. Most would be dead. Some would just lay down their arms and disappear into the civilian population and some might have escaped to... Ireland? But there just didn't seem to be any plans for massive prisoner-of-war camps to house this defeated army. But of course Britain didn't just roll over, and Hitler concluded he couldn't gain air superiority in the skies of Britain, so he turned his attention to the east and Russia.

Here the record is clear. At first the German advance into Russia went swiftly and successfully. Russian soldiers were reluctant to surrender and would usually fight to the death. Nevertheless, Russian prisoners began to accumulate in such great numbers by 1942 that the Germans decided it was time to organize formal POW compounds. The Germans were highly conscious of rank and soon had prison camps for officers, other camps for non-commissioned officers, and for the unlucky soldiers of lower ranks they developed forced labor camps. Camps began to spring up all over Germany. Before the war was over allied prisoners were held in over 50 camps of all sorts. As the numbers of allied prisoners grew the Germans felt the need to further subdivide the camps into those holding army prisoners that were run by the Wehrmacht and those holding airmen that were run by the Luftwaffe. Hitler had expected to take prisoners on the ground but the influx of prisoners that it seems the Germans had never expected, came from the air. Goering had assured Hitler that the Luftwaffe would never be conquered. He had never dreamed that a thousand planes would arrive at the end of May 1942 and "dehouse" 45,000 residents of Cologne. He was devastated in July of 1943 when over 800 bombers released their firestorm on Hamburg, and when American P-51 fighters first appeared over Berlin in March of 1944, Goering is said to have admitted, "The jig was up." The Germans had simply never imagined the devastation that would be rained upon them from the skies over the Fatherland.

The U.S. alone flew nearly 1.7 *million* missions against Germany during WWII. Flying these missions were over 32,000 combat aircraft of which over 17,000 were lost in action. From these planes over 43,000 airmen were killed or wounded and an astounding 51,000 went down over German-held territory. Some managed to evade capture and a lot were just listed as missing in action but the vast majority of these 51,000 became prisoners of war. They were unwanted guests that had not been invited to Germany but now they must be housed.

In October of 1942 Stalag Luft 1 was opened at Barth, Germany, a small cold little town on the Baltic Sea. The camp held allied airmen of various ranks but it being the German nature to separate men by rank, in September of 1943 they opened Stalag Luft 6 to house the NCOs and separate them from the officers who were left at Stalag Luft I. Unfortunately this camp was located in what is now Lithuania and the overwhelming image the survivors recall is that they were always cold and hungry. But even this camp couldn't house the now burgeoning numbers of airmen, so in May of 1944 another camp was opened in Gross Tychow, Pomerania, an area in northern Poland. Officially its name was *Kriegsgefangenenlager der Luftwaffe 4 Grosstychow*, but it was usually just known as Stalag Luft 4. It wasn't situated nearly as far east as Stalag Luft 6 so in the late spring of 1944, as the Russians were advancing from the east, it was decided to move the inmates of Stalag Luft 6 to the newly opened Stalag Luft 4. This migration of captured airmen is a horror story of the worst sort.

On the afternoon of July 14, 1944 the American camp leader was advised that the first 2000 men were to be shipped out the next day. They could each take two Red Cross food parcels and as much personal luggage as they could haul. On the morning of July 15 they began a strict three-mile march to a train station where the men were packed into airless boxcars and shipped to the port of Memel. There, the first 1700 were crammed into the *Insterburg*, an old coal hauler that was so crowded the men could not even lie down. Being mid-July the heat down in the cargo hold was oppressive. There was no water or suitable toilet facilities. Down in the dark airless holds men passed out, others became seasick. The nightmare seemed endless. Of course the men were not told where they were going or how long it would take. If they were going to Germany they would be taken by train, wouldn't they? Where were they going in this sweltering old rust bucket? Rumors spread that the ship was to be scuttled with all aboard. Hour after hour their steamy misery grew worse and it certainly was compounded by the lack of an obvious destination. After about 40 hours they arrived on the Baltic coast of Germany at Swinemunde where they were once again packed back into cattle cars. By now most of them had been separated from their luggage and it is no surprise that the promises that the luggage would come later, were never kept. Many were without food or water and ready to pass out. It must be remembered that these were not healthy boys who had just been shot down. Many had spent months or years in POW camps and already lost 30% of their normal body weight before their transport began. It was the heat of July as they marched under the sun, baked in the steamship, and roasted in the cattle cars. After a total of about three days on the move, the train doors were thrown open as they arrived at Grosstychow in what is now Poland. Unfortunately the train tracks didn't run to Stalag Luft 4 but ended some distance from the camp. Today it is difficult to assess just how far away the camp was, as estimates and reports vary from two to six kilometers. The best guess seems to be about two miles—two very long miles that turned into a gauntlet that these men would never forget.

    As they spilled out of the train they were met by *Hauptmann* (Captain) Walter Pickhardt who was responsible for security at Stalag Luft 4. He was a real bastard. His nickname was "The Beast of Berlin." His mug shot looks like a round-faced Anthony Hopkins, with his hair slicked back, during his portrayal of Hannibal Lecter in *Silence of the Lambs*. Walter Pickhardt was simply an evil human being. One prisoner, C.A. Room, described him as, "Overdressed, brutal-eyed, fleshy faced, twitching with excitement and leaving no one in doubt that he was in charge of events." As the dazed and confused POWs came tumbling from the railcars he began shouting at the men that they were to pick up what belongings they might still have and run off down a dirt road that tunneled through the stunted Polish forest. Most of the men were still handcuffed. Weakened from their ordeal on the ship and trains, they could not keep up the pace. The trail was lined with guards who were taunted by Pickhardt to keep this chain of men moving down the gauntlet through the forest. Captain Pickhardt inflamed the guards by reminding them that these *terrorflieger* were paid a bonus for all of the women and children they had killed with their bombs.

In the midst of this group stood *Feldwebel* (Sergeant) Hans Schmidt. He must have looked like Goliath. Accounts of his size vary from 6'2" to "at least seven feet tall." His weight was reported from 210 to 300 pounds. He had a huge head with a long scar running down the left side of his face, an unusually mean sneer, a ruddy complexion, and a big bony nose. He also had the biggest set of hands any of the men had ever seen. He was such a mean son-of-a-bitch that he figures prominently in the journals, stories, and reminiscences of any airman unfortunate enough to have crossed his path. He was simply known as "Big Stoop" and he was universally feared and despised. One of his favorite abuses was to slap a man on the ear as hard as he could. This would usually send the man flying and rupture his eardrum all in the same motion. Numerous men lost their hearing in ears that had been destroyed by Big Stoop. He was the sort of bastard that would beat prisoners for the most minor of infractions and, if he were in the mood, for no reason at all he would just slug men out of meanness. He roamed up and down this parade of jogging, exhausted prisoners dealing out his viscous little doses of meanness everywhere he went. If the men slowed down he would order the guards to bayonet them. These hungry, dehydrated men were exhausted by now and most of them just dumped their luggage in order to keep up the pace. One after another they were bayoneted for failure to do so. Sometimes they were stabbed in the legs but mostly it was in the buttocks. After having endured this abuse from the guards this long train of prisoners was soon joined by a pack of German police dogs. Pickhardt took great delight in turning the dogs loose on anybody who fell behind. The biggest dog, seemingly the leader of the pack, was an especially mean dog someone called "Teufel." The dog would just sink his teeth into a man's butt or legs and shake him like a rag doll until finally called off.

By the time the gauntlet had been run, many men had dog bites to go with their multiple bayonet wounds, and, unbelievably, two poor souls had more than 50 wounds each by the time they reached camp. The official record shows 228 men with wounds and/or dog bites that needed treatment. The next day the second contingent of prisoners arrived, and as they met Pickhardt, Big Stoop, Teufel, and the rest of the welcoming committee, they received 77 bayonet wounds, 8 dog bites, and 29 had blows from rifle butts as they made their way to camp. Most of these men would report that this was the longest two miles of their lives. For many of the men who survived until the end of hostilities they would remember this as one of the ugliest experiences of the entire war. It became infamously known as "The Run Up The Road."

Upon arrival at Stalag Luft 4 the men were not interred, rather they were held outside for 24 hours as they underwent "examinations." Those with bites, beatings, or stab wounds were seen by a German doctor. Everyone was thoroughly strip searched to make sure no contraband would be taken into camp. Those few men who had been strong enough to keep a grip on some of their possessions as they made the trip now had everything taken away for "safety's sake." During the course of these searches Captain Pickhardt would threaten to shoot any of the guards who didn't show sufficient zest in mistreating the allied prisoners. Witnesses watched as Big Stoop "picked up one American prisoner, held him in the air and slammed him down. He then poked this prisoner in the stomach with his fist and sent the American spinning across the room where he doubled up against the wall." Their journey had become a piece of living hell.

It's hard to imagine anyone looking forward to a prisoner-of-war camp but after their ordeal in transit, when the gates were thrown open, the allied prisoners from Stalag Luft 6 were happy to be "home" in their new camp, Stalag Luft 4.

Stalag Luft 4 was divided into four compounds or "lagers," named A, B, C and D, plus the main vorlagar which included the infirmary, as well as food and clothing storerooms. (More lagers were added later.) Each lager was designed to accommodate 1600 prisoners. (By February of 1945 each housed 2,500). The Spartan barracks were standard wooden German barracks. Each was about 40' X 130' and they were divided into rooms of about 15' X 23' that held 8 wooden bunk beds. The beds were crudely built with six wooden slats supporting a "mattress," a large paper bag filled with wood shavings. A small table, some wooden benches and a small coke stove completed the furnishings. Toilet facilities were a pit latrine and the wash huts had no running water other than an outdoor hand pump. The entire camp was then surrounded by double barbed wire fences, guard towers, and the ever-present dogs. Everything was minimal.

Escape from Stalag Luft 4 was never really a consideration as the camp was opened half way through 1944 and emptied about 7 months later at the beginning of 1945. It was located so far from any allied territory that evasion would have been next to impossible if one was to attempt to make it to Switzerland or Spain. Perhaps one could have made it to a Baltic port and found a ship headed for Sweden but it also must be remembered that nearly everyone who was interned in Stalag Luft 4 arrived there after D-Day and with the knowledge that the Russians were advancing from the east. The best survival strategy seemed to be to just sit it out until eventual liberation.

In July of 1944 when the influx arrived from Stalag Luft 6, a full camp society began to organize and develop. Everyone got their own bed and personal space. They also began to fit in with the other guys and form friendships and little groups. A society began to develop as the routine of camp life began to settle in. It became very important for each prisoner to have a friend, someone to share the misery with, someone who would listen to your stories and share all the rumors that were to become as common as the lice.

But all the news was not necessarily born of rumor. The *"kriegies"* (*kriegsgefangenen* is German for "prisoner of war") as the prisoners became known, were a resourceful lot and the one thing they had plenty of was time: time to dream, time to scheme, and time to invent. It seems as if in all of the Stalags in Nazi Germany the prisoners managed to construct radios. Certain guards could be bribed for tiny components, and things got smuggled in. Next to the components the next most important factor was technical expertise. John Bossley from the 459th bomb group was the man with the skills in Stalag Luft 4. After searching the camp for the most qualified person it was decided to trust their precious components to Bossley; he knew radios. They got him transferred into Lager "D" where they had collected all the tiny electronic bits. Bossley spent night after night in the cookhouse working on his project until he finally had it working. News! What a thrill, but the next problem was where to hide the tiny radio as German "ferrets" were always keeping an eye out for any suspicious activities or objects. After many thoughtful ideas were considered, that first radio ended up living inside of a softball that was carefully unstitched and re-stitched every night! A later radio in Stalag Luft 4 came in three parts. It was assembled every night and the BBC would be tuned in. The next morning the war news would be whispered around and this precious little electronic umbilical to home was then disassembled in three tiny pieces with one third being given to a different *kreige*. They would walk all day with their tiny treasure and then each night they would reassemble this little lifeline to the real world.

On June 6th, they were ecstatic. The *kriegies* knew of D-Day before the guards did. They were still in Stalag Luft 6 and had already known that the Russians were closing in from the east. As the summer wore on they knew of Patton's race to Paris and the liberation of France. They all dreamed they would be home by Christmas.

Next to the Germans the biggest enemy of the prisoners was time. There was simply nothing to do. They would get up and fall in for roll call. The guards would count them to make sure no one had disappeared during the night. The men would then go back to the barracks and wait for one man to bring a pot of ersatz coffee made from burned barley and a slice of black "bread." They called it bread and it looked a bit like bread but it contained woodchips, bits of straw, and a lot of things that men were thankful they couldn't recognize. On rare occasions they would receive Red Cross parcels that would have Spam, dried milk, raisins, prunes, a can of butter, crackers, soap, cigarettes and assorted little treats. Unfortunately each parcel was usually split between 4 men and their contents didn't go very far. They clearly were on starvation rations. Some men reported losing a pound a day for their duration in the POW camps. The average *kreige* lost 30% of his body weight during incarceration. The one thing that was always on their mind was *food*. It is interesting to note that there were several thousand men, all in their teens, 20s, or 30s who had not seen a woman in months, yet they reported that they never had thoughts or dreams of sex. It was always *food*.

In the evening there were often boiled potatoes or turnips, but never enough. It was followed by everyone falling in to be recounted, then off to the barracks where they were bolted in for the night with their empty stomachs.

In the middle of June of 1944, a tragic incident took place at Stalag Luft 4 that was so ugly it brought the camp commandant up before the war crime tribunals in August of 1945. As Clem Pine understands it, the commandant had gone home on leave only to find several of his family members had been killed in an air raid. He was absolutely infuriated. Nearly all of the men held in Stalag Luft 4 were members of the air force and almost all had had a role in the bombing of Germany. They were the hated *luft gangsters*, the *terrorfliegers* that had systematically reduced the magnificent German cities, the charming little German towns, and now his own German family, to rubble. In a rage the commandant stormed into camp looking for blood.

The guards, without exception, had enforced all of the rules of Stalag Luft 4. Still, there was a certain understanding between the *kriegies* and the guards concerning just how far you could bend a rule. Just such a rule was: No one may enter or leave a barrack through a window. It was a silly rule as there was no place to go if you went through a window, and as these young men were mostly fairly athletic they would often just hop out of a window rather than going out and around to the front door. Everyone knew the rule but the guards never made much of a fuss about it, and they usually just looked the other way if they saw a guy hop out the window. Unfortunately for Technical Sergeant Ralph "Aubrey" Teague, the day he chose to jump out of the window was the day the enraged camp commandant returned infuriated by the loss of his family members. He seems to have issued orders that any violation of any camp rule would result in the violator being shot dead on the spot.

June 19, 1944, was the fateful day. At about 3:30 that afternoon Teague hopped out of the window and wasn't even going anywhere. An armed guard was about 50 yards away and just stared at Teague as he emerged from the window. Clearly the guard didn't want to shoot. He had his orders but he must have been severely conflicted as he waited almost five full minutes before he raised his rife and fired. The bullet entered Teague just over his left arm and emerged from his back. Teague survived the gunshot wound but as he lay on the ground the Germans refused to help him and it is believed he simply bled to death.

The incident left a pall over the camp for the next few days. The story was told and retold for the rest of the life of Stalag Luft 4. When Clem arrived five months later it was one of the first things he learned about life as a POW. Life was tenuous, life was cheap, and you had better watch your step if you had any hope of surviving the ordeal.

During the summer of 1944 these *kriegies* would do their best to organize sporting events but the Germans were stingy with equipment. There were a few treasured books to be read and passed around and some well-worn decks of cards.

Boredom was the enemy. A few men saved up their raisins, set them to fermenting, and soon had lousy raisin wine. Some guys saved their Red Cross milk cans and used them to build little one-burner stoves. Some days they would be lucky enough to be assigned KP duty where they would have something to do, and they probably could steal some food.

Summer turned to autumn and the war news had the allies moving slowly across France. As winter approached there was a new enemy to contend with: The Cold.

Each man had pants and a shirt. Many had overcoats and each had a pair of shoes. Luck had a lot to do with the shoes they received and if they didn't get a good fitting pair 1945 was going to bring them Hell. Each man had a couple of army blankets and that was it. When the cold set in they would sleep with their buddy to share some precious body heat.

And the climate gods were angry. The winter of 1944-1945 was one of the coldest of the century in Europe. Men never got warm. Men had frost bight that turned gangrenous and they lost limbs. Many men froze to death.

Into Stalag Luft 4, into this hideous winter, Clem Pine was about to be deposited.

CHAPTER 8
LIFE IN A PRISON CAMP

The grim ugliness of Stalag Luft 4.

As the old Polish steam engine belched its way north across Pomerania the world turned bleak. It was now well into November and all the leaves were gone. The greens had turned to yellow, passed through red and fallen to the earth to rot into grayness. The naked trees began to look sinister. The sky was a dismal ashen gray. There were patches of dirty gray snow on the ground and the trees became more stunted the farther north they chugged. Clem had been shot out of the sky on August 16, during the summer. He had spent the autumn of 1944 in various German hospitals that had been relatively friendly with clean white sheets. He had made good friends, eaten good food, and known the sound of laughter. All in all, he had been treated very well. He was well aware of how close he had come to losing his leg. It certainly would have been amputated if it weren't for the kindness and professionalism of that one German doctor. But now he was leaving that world and chugging into this colorless, bitter, frozen world. The few people who could be seen in the countryside were all bundled up in their colorless garments and looked mean. Maybe they weren't mean, just unhappy. They were living miserable lives, in this miserable countryside, in this miserable winter, of this miserable war. Their lives were miserable and *they* were the free people! Clem was heading to a POW camp.

The guards on the train had been regular guys. They were friendly enough, but as the filthy steam engine chugged to a stop the atmosphere in the train changed dramatically. Everyone became silent; a foreboding crept through the train, and then came the dreaded sound of SS jackboots. "Friendly" was a word Clem could leave out of his vocabulary for a long time to come.

These SS guards in their starkly black uniforms marched into their carriage and promptly took over. The regular guards were dismissed with one whiff of the hand and growling, barking orders were shouted at Clem and the other ten prisoners he had arrived with. In an instant he was standing in this barren, bleak forest and looking down a long dirt road. Down THE long dirt road. Down the road that would be infamous for evermore as the location of "The Run Up The Road" that had occurred here four months earlier. Sixty years later the word Clem Pine repeats over and over when describing this world is "bleak." Everything from the sky, to the stunted forest, to the gray dirt, was bleak. But what had become bleakest of all was Clem's life, and he full well knew it.

Due to the fact that there were only a handful of prisoners arriving that day, the full-fledged "welcoming committee" was not there to greet them. The SS guards began to herd this little group of scared men down the road through the forest to who knows where. They expected to find a POW camp but knew full well they also could simply be shot. On they trudged, until suddenly there before them in the wide open was the shocking ugliness of Stalag Luft 4. Guard towers, barbed wire, machine guns, police dogs—it was all there—straight from their worst nightmare. This was now to be "home."

They were marched into a big hall to be strip-searched. In their freezing nakedness they were gone over with a fine-toothed comb. Their hair was searched, their cavities were searched, and every bit of clothing right down to each seam was searched. On top of being scared to death from being thrown into this horrifying world, now they were being humiliated by all the nakedness and probing. It was then that they saw him. Sauntering their way with that huge, ugly scar, those mammoth hands, and the gargantuan frame, came all the meanness of Big Stoop. Clem recalls, "Out of the corner of my eye I was watching him like a hawk. You could just see he was brimming with meanness and just looking for an excuse to light into somebody."

Somebody told them to get dressed. Clem was sitting on a wooden bench putting his clothes back on when *Wham!* Big Stoop had smacked the guy next to him half way across the room. He lay there bleeding out of his ear as Big Stoop bellowed, "Don't put your feet on the furniture." The poor guy had only been trying to tie his shoes, when he had put his foot on the bench.

Prisoners coming "up the road" and about to enter camp.

It had been an enlightening introduction to Stalag Luft 4, Clem's new home.

By now Stalag Luft 4 was well past being over-crowded. Since the mass of prisoners had arrived from Stalag Luft 6, four months before, there had been a steady addition of these small groups such as Clem had been part of. Planes were being shot down every single day at this point in the war, so almost daily there were more men pouring into this ever-swelling camp.

Clem was read the rules of the camp and led off to Lager B and his assigned barrack. As he arrived, rather than being greeted warmly by fellow airmen who could sympathize with his shock of arrival, he felt an icy coldness as he entered the stark wooden shed. This room that had been built for 16, already housed 22, and one more would just make things worse. He was not very welcome. Bleak.

Clem arrived with a good pair of military pants, a British battle jacket, an overcoat, and luckily, a good fitting pair of shoes. When he had left the hospital the captain had warned him to protect his injured leg, so he had cut up a pair of long johns that he wore to support his bad leg. That and his two blankets were it. His "luggage" didn't take up much room but there still was no welcome mat out to greet him. He had no bunk, just one of the wood shaving "mattresses" that were of little value, and those two blankets, to get him through the long nights of the coldest winter Poland had seen in decades. Yes, bleak.

During that first week in camp two things overcame Clem. The first was the cold. It was just always cold, just so damn cold. The second was warmth, the warmth of friendship. Clem met another miserable airman and they began to buddy up. Charles Croty, better known as "Shorty," was from Boston, and like Clem, he needed a friend.

Shorty had been a tail gunner in a B-24 that was shot down over Czechoslovakia. He and his crewmates had bailed out and were captured as soon as they hit the ground not far from where the big bomber had crashed and started quite a fire. The enraged locals who captured these terrified airmen marched them to the scene of this burning wreckage, forced them to take off their shoes and socks, and then marched them right through the burning debris. Shorty's scarred feet and legs were not all that different from Clem's wounded leg. Sharing similar experiences, they soon were telling stories and playing cards. Shorty taught Clem the game of cribbage and they would spend hours on the floor of their hut where they had drilled a cribbage board in the floor. Their major activity though was walking. They would walk 'round and 'round their lager for hours on end. Mostly they did it to ward off the cold but Clem also knew that he had to rehabilitate his bad leg if it was ever to regain its full strength. Little did he know that these hours of walking, days of walking, weeks of walking, were getting him in shape for the longest, coldest, most miserable walk of his life, but daily his leg was growing stronger.

The men were always looking for any diversion they could find to kill the time. It was too cold for most sports but some guy came up with the idea of throwing buckets of water down a walking path and creating a long sheet of ice. Soon the guys were sprinting full speed to the ice and sliding away on their bellies, butts, or whatever. It brought some much-needed laughter and got them through one more long, cold day, but that constant gnawing hunger always remained. Amazingly, these guys could even turn their hunger into an activity that would pass the time. They began listing foods. One day, as they walked, they would spend an entire afternoon listing all the kinds of soups that they could remember. The next morning they would be at it again but this time it would be cookies, or maybe pies, or vegetables, or meat dishes. It was an activity that killed a lot of time and it also reminded the guys of home and something to look forward to. Most importantly, it must have given them hope.

Prisoners entering camp. Note the guard dogs.

Killing time with a baseball game.

As the winter wore on, the POWs, the *kriegies*, had so much time on their hands that they began to dream up ways to make life miserable for their captors. It didn't make any difference which side of the barbed wire they lived on, everyone knew that the war was coming to an end and it was just a matter of time before authority would be exchanged. It emboldened the *kriegies*.

One of Clem's fellow prisoners, a man from Alabama, told the following story:

> There was a fellow in C lager who was from Texas, a little short fellow, but he spoke Russian and several other

languages, and he worked in the Vorlager each day and would come back in at night. One day he was coming back in to C lager and there were some Russians standing out there, about twenty or thirty of them, so he just spoke to the Russians (in Russian I presume), called them to attention, marched up to the gate and the German opened the gate and he took the Russians in. We got them in there and distributed them out among the barracks. Very hurriedly, we got them cleaned up and cut their hair, shaved their faces and put them in American uniforms. We had an escape committee in the prison. Usually at roll call, there would be people missing, but then after we got those Russians in there, and got them in American uniforms, they counted us and that day there were more people, instead of fewer. It was too late in the afternoon at the last roll call (in the dead of winter up there, it was about three o'clock in the afternoon and it starts getting dark about 3:30 or 4:00). So they just put us in the barracks and locked the doors. They had huge wooden shutters made out of 2X4s that they closed over the windows and put a bar over it. If those barracks were to have caught fire, we would all have been burned to a crisp. The following day, we came out for roll call at daybreak and still had too many people, so the Germans set up a table in the middle of the compound and put everybody on one side of the compound, and they would call your name. We had a little thing called "Kriegy," dog tags, which were POW dog tags with our number on it. The Germans had a card on each one of us with that number on the card and our name and this sort of thing, plus a picture of us. So as they would call our names, we would walk out into the middle of the compound and then show them our dog tags. They'd check that number against the number on the cards, and they'd check our pictures. Then we'd walk over to the other side. What they were trying to do was find out who these extra people were and to isolate them over there. So we did everything we could to slow down the process. You'd make them call your name about ten times before you'd ever go walking out there and if they'd start raising cain with you, you'd say, "Well, I just couldn't understand you when you called my name." So, on up in the middle of the afternoon, we had about a thousand people over on the other side of the compound (about fifty percent of us). It was obvious that they weren't going to get through. Then we started passing the word along on both sides to start making snowballs. So each side started making big piles of snowballs and then started throwing snowballs at each other. Then somebody yelled "Charge!" Both sides of the compound charged and ran together and everybody got mixed up. Well, the upshot of that was that even the day I got liberated, several months later, there still were a couple of those Russians with the group I was in. The Germans were just too damned dumb to ever be able to handle a situation like that.

Roll Call.

As November drifted into December the thermometer continued its slide. Nights became more miserable, hot food more appealing, and the rumor of being home by Christmas more remote. Then true disaster struck. A week before Christmas the nightly BBC news funneled through the tiny radios and crushed the hopes and dreams of every POW in every prison camp in Germany. The German offensive that would become known as "The Battle of the Bulge" was on. The steady allied advanced across the Rhine was stopped cold. For the first time since any prisoner had been locked up in Stalag Luft 4 the Germans were on the offensive. The Germans were actually "winning" this one piece of the war. Soon the Guards were giddy with their "good" news. They were quick to let all the *kriegies* know that the Germans were once again on the move and "winning" the war. It simply made the bleak prison existence that much bleaker.

Today Clem recalls that all of the POWs knew that this offensive would not last—the Germans were not about to win the war—but they all realized that this meant that their liberation was going to be postponed by this reversal of fortunes. It didn't make the Christmas of 1944 very merry.

One of the overriding memories of those soldiers who fought in the Battle of the Bulge was their life and death struggle with the cold. Their stories are legendary, how they battled frostbite as much as the Wehrmacht. It was the most brutal winter anyone in Europe could remember. The conditions were absolutely abominable. What has seldom been mentioned in the history books is the toll that same winter was taking on all of the half-starved POWs all over Europe as they huddled in their wooden shacks with two blankets. At least the POWs were indoors, but they were so underfed that maintaining minimum metabolism was problematic. Cold and starvation are not competitive events, so it makes no sense to evaluate comparative miseries. That winter of 1944 was stamping its unforgettable meanness on everybody's Merry Christmas.

What was a comparative misery that could be evaluated was the treatment POWs were receiving from their captors in the various countries around the world. To be a captive of the Russians was a truly awful fate. They were ruthless with their prisoners. To be captured by the Japanese was even worse. After the war, the unspeakable horror described by survivors of the Japanese camps made every prisoner of the Germans thankful that no matter how bad conditions had been, their treatment had been far more humane than that received by prisoners of the Japanese. Christmas of 1944 was a good example.

The Germans as well as the allies were suffering greatly from the cold, but nevertheless it was Christmas. To the amazement of the men hunkered down in the frozen misery of Stalag Luft 4, on Christmas Eve the Germans began a Red Cross parcel distribution. This time, however, rather than dividing a parcel between four men, each man got his own eleven-pound parcel! Joy to the World! What a wonderful Christmas present that each and every one of these men would remember for the rest of their lives. Food, glorious food! Hallelujah!

Then the Germans negotiated an agreement, that on this one night only, the prisoners would not be locked in their barracks but would be free to roam around camp, if on their honor, there would be no escape attempts or monkey business. It was a deal. An infectious Christmas spirit began to diffuse through the camp. Bundled-up groups of cold, cheerful men began wandering from barrack to barrack, singing Christmas carols while hugging their precious Red Cross parcels. Friends exchanged Christmas "presents" from their parcels. Each parcel came with a miniature game of some sort. Perhaps it was a tiny chess set or a deck of cards. Some had a fold-up cribbage board, or board games of some sort, but they all had some delightful little diversion to help cope with the mind-numbing boredom of the long winter.

Little groups of men would gather and all contribute something from their parcel that would be made into a communal dish such as bread pudding. Those who had turned their raisins and prunes into "wine" were proud to share a sip with their comrades. It wasn't a proper Christmas dinner, but under the circumstances it came pretty darn close. For the first time in memory everyone had enough food to eat their fill.

When "dinner" was over the men drifted back out into the cold and found themselves again joining little groups of carolers. As the night wore on they exhausted their repertoire of Christmas carols but, before turning in, the British *kriegies* gathered around a candle for one last song:

My country 'tis of thee, sweet land of liberty, Of thee we sing:
Land where my fathers died, Land of the pilgrims' pride.
From every mountainside,
Let freedom ring!
My native country, thee,
Land of the noble, free, Thy name I love.
I love the rocks and hills, Thy woods and templed hills;
My heart with rapture thrills, Like that above.

Let music swell the breeze, And ring from all the trees, sweet freedom's song; Let mortal tongues awake; Let all that breathe

partake; Let rocks their silence break,
  The sound prolong.

  Our fathers' God, to Thee, Author of liberty, To Thee we sing.
  Long may our land be bright, With freedom's holy light,
  Protect us by Thy might,
  Great God, our King!

And if the Germans thought it was just one more Christmas carol... so be it.

Northwest of Stalag Luft 4, at Barth, the site of Stalag Luft 1, another Christmas story was unfolding. Earl Wassom an ex-POW tells the story:

In war-time, a place called Barth was Hell. It was a prisoner-of-war camp located only a few miles south of the Baltic Sea in Northern Germany. Downed aircrews were interned there after having been shot down and captured by the enemy. Ten thousand were held there as prisoners.

One on-going "high" occurred when each new contingent of "guests" arrived in the camp. Up-to-date, uncensored information became immediately available. The reports brought in by these new POWs gave fresh, unbiased running accounts of how the war was progressing on both the Eastern Front with the Russians and on the Western Front.

The increasing numbers of bombers and fighters appearing in the air overhead brought silent but exuberant joy and hope to Barth's imprisoned. As optimism flourished small group conversation centered on the war's end and their freedom. Liberation was on everyone's lips. The war was indeed winding down! Talk of being home for Christmas became a Utopian Dream.

Although all embraced the Dream, not all were optimistic. This difference in opinion brought about the "Bet at Barth." A wager was on. New life came to the camp. But what was there to wager!? There was no money, no freedom of 3-day passes to London, no material possessions for the loser to forfeit, no points or promotions to be gained or lost.

In a heated conversation two men got carried away in their claims. An optimistic airman bet a pessimistic one on the following terms: "If we aren't home by Christmas, I will kiss your a** before the whole group formation right after headcount on Christmas morning." They shook hands. The bet was on!

Well, the optimist hadn't counted on the Battle of the Bulge in early December. Consequently, the war was prolonged and they were still in Barth on Christmas Day, 1944. Christmas morning was cold, there was snow on the ground and frigid air was blowing in off the Baltic Sea. The body count for the compound began, each man was counted off: ein..., zwei..., drei..., vier..., funf..., sechs..., sieben..., acht...

Under ordinary circumstances, when the counting was completed and the German guards were satisfied that everyone was accounted for, the group split up and everyone went to their barracks. But this time, everybody stayed in formation. The two betting "Kriegies" walked out of the formation and went into the barracks. No one else moved! The guards were puzzled. They didn't know what was going on.

Soon, the two men came back out of the barracks. One was carrying a bucket of water with a towel over the other arm. The second one marched to the front of the formation, turned his back toward the assembled troops and guards, pulled down his pants and stooped over. The other took the towel, dipped it in the soapy water and washed his posterior. The whole formation was standing there looking and laughing. The German guards and dignitaries of Barth stood gazing in amazement, they didn't know what was going on. Then the optimist bent over and kissed his opponent on the rear! A mighty cheer went up from over 2,000 men. Then the puzzled guards joined in the fun.

Nothing changed on Christmas day—the same black bread and thin soup, sparse and flavorless. As evening fell, the weather worsened, the barracks were cold, the last of the daily allotted coal briquettes were reduced to nothing but white ash. Boredom was setting in and the prisoners anticipated another long, miserable night. Suddenly, the door opened... a voice shouted, "The curfew has been lifted for tonight! We're going to have a Christmas service over in the next compound." The weather was bitterly cold, the new fallen snow crunched under the feet of the men as they quickly shuffled toward their congregating comrades in the distance.

The nightly curfew always kept men inside—this Christmas night's reprieve allowed them to be outside after dark for the first time. Above, the stars were shining brightly and were high in the northern skies; the dim flicker of Aurora Borealis added a magical touch as the troops assembled. Gratitude was felt in their hearts... a lone singer led out with one of the world's most familiar and loved carols. Others joined in and soon there was joyful worship ringing throughout the camp.

Silent night! Holy night!
All is calm, all is bright...

The German guards marching their assigned beats stopped

in their tracks... they turned their heads toward the music. The words were unfamiliar but they recognized the tune... after all, Stille Nacht, Heilige Nacht was composed by a German. They loosened up, smiled, and joined in the celebration; the praise became bilingual.

> Round yon virgin mother and Child
> Cinsam wacht nurdas traute hoch heilige Paar
>
> Holy Infant so tender and mild
> Holder Knabe im lockigen Hoiar
>
> Sleep in heavenly peace. Sleep in heavenly peace.
> Schlaf in himmlischer ruh! Schlaf in himmlischer ruh.

The Bet at Barth had paid off. Everyone had won! As the words of the carol rang in their hearts, there was a literal fulfillment. Tonight they would sleep in peace. War and internment did not have the power to destroy the meaning and beauty of this special day.

Back at Stalag Luft 4 Clem and his buddies were beginning to pay the price for their over indulgence. Digestive systems that had adjusted to bits of black bread and potatoes just couldn't cope with the sudden influx of eleven pounds of food from the Red Cross! So on Christmas morning when children across the world were rushing to find what Santa had left in their stockings, Clem and his friends were all rushing to the latrines to relieve themselves of the previous night's celebration. A diarrhea epidemic had set in with such ferocity that many men couldn't possibly wait for their turn and resorted to filling those Red Cross parcel boxes that had brought them so much joy the night before. Such is the plight of prisoners of war.

As Christmas receded it was back to battling the cold. The new year brought no joy. It reminded them all that the idea they would be home for Christmas had only been a dream and nothing more. The German advance was still strong as the Battle of the Bulge progressed and of course the guards were quick to remind them how the tide had turned. By the middle of January, however, the German offensive had collapsed, and once again the Americans were on the move. The guards became sullen and the *kriegies* were not shy about reminding them that now it was only a matter of time before the American Army would roll across Germany and be entering Berlin.

Note the new brick construction.
This is the "cooler" being built.

Clem had a Jewish friend in camp. His name was Dave Kimmel and he had an extraordinary hatred of the Germans. Although they had yet to learn about Auschwitz and the rest of the extermination camps, they were well aware of all the anti-Semitic hatred toward the Jews that Hitler had been whipping up even before the war started. Dave had spent a lot of time in the "cooler," the isolation cells, for giving the finger to some especially annoying guard and complimenting his gesture with a warm, "Fuck Hitler!"

Every night when the *kriegies* were all locked into their barracks the Germans would turn loose the guard dogs to patrol the camp as an insurance policy against escape. Had anyone managed to extricate himself from the barracks and make a dash in the dark for the fences, the dogs would have torn him to pieces, especially Teufel, the biggest and meanest of the pack. There may have been some animal lovers among the POWs but they universally hated and despised that pack of vicious animals ever since their encounter with them on "The Run Up The Road."

At the front of each of the barracks was a little entryway that had a small window. Sometimes in the evening after everyone was locked in for the night the *kriegies* would go out into that entry area and open the little window to get a bit of fresh air or have a cigarette. One especially cold January night, Clem and Dave Kimmel went out there for a smoke. They were sharing a cigarette when Dave opened the window to flick out an ash. No sooner did he open it than he ducked down quietly and scuttled back to Clem. "Shhhhhhhhhh, there is a dog curled up right under the window!" And with that Dave disappeared back into his room. Clem knew that Dave had a streak of evil in him and wondered what was up. He crept over to the window and sure enough there lay the big dog. With the bitter cold, Teufel had curled up next to the door, trying to get a bit of warmth from the building. In a minute Dave was back. On the stove in his room there had been a big can of water boiling. Dave quietly stuck it out the window and dumped it. "EEYOWIEEEEEE!" Teufel shot off like a rocket, yelping as if he had just had a pot of boiling water poured on him.

In just a few minutes they could hear the guards going around from barrack to barrack raising hell everywhere they went. They came crashing into Clem's barrack, where of course, no one knew anything about the scalded dog. They ripped pictures from the wall, dumped out boxes and knocked everything off the table. It was total mayhem. Clem says when they left it looked like a hand grenade had gone off in their room. Nobody minded the mess, however, as they all were now doubled over in laughter enjoying the whole affair.

As January ground on and the news from the BBC lifted their spirits, it was obvious just the opposite was happening to guards. They were all aware of the allies' advance across Germany from the west. Of much greater concern to the Germans, however, was the Russian army that was now fast approaching from the east. The Russians were absolutely ruthless and every German soldier knew it. To a man, they all knew that when the war ended they would far prefer that their fate be determined by the Americans or British rather than the Russians. Maybe it was time to be nice to all these American and British POWs.

It must be remembered that the vast majority of the men in Stalag Luft 4 at this time had previously been held in Stalag Luft 6. When the Russians had approached that camp they clearly remembered the horrors of being moved in mass to a new camp. It had just been six months since their ordeal in that decrepit ship and "The Run Up The Road." So, although the day of liberation was drawing nearer, things were getting a bit tense, and rumors began to fly. There was talk every day about the possibility of a forced march. This was still mid January and Northern Poland was still tightly held in the icy grip of winter. Sub-zero temperatures were common that winter but still the men knew that if there was to be a forced march they had better get in shape for it. For a couple of months they had been hunkered down, just enduring the cold. Now they began to walk. If they could stand the cold they would walk all day long. Now those good-fitting shoes began to become one of Clem's most valuable possessions. He and Shorty once again began to walk for hours and hours. And the rumors kept flying; clearly *something* was about to happen. That nightly link to the BBC reassured everyone that these rumors had some merit. They full well knew the Russians were near. Then toward the end of January the dull rumble of artillery could be heard to the east. At first the men couldn't be sure, but soon there was no doubt. The eastern front was approaching just as fast, and just as surely, as February.

Organizing the men for a march.

CHAPTER 9
THE DEATH MARCH

By the end of January 1945 the outcome of the war was no longer in doubt. The German offensive at the Battle of the Bulge had died and with it went all hopes of defeating the allied advance from the west. The Germans simply had no significant military resources left. The Russians were pinching in from the east and the only real question was how long could the remaining Germans hold out?

Every German from Hitler on down must have been playing out the end game in his own mind. Hitler and several of his top generals must have known that their fate was either a humiliating trial in the dock, as war criminals, or they could avoid it all via suicide. Others must have been making plans to flee to South America or some other safe haven. For the lower ranks it was a fight to the death, surrender to the enemy, or try to dissolve back into the civilian population. Whatever the rank, each man surely must have spent hours and hours thinking about how it all would end. That surely must also have been true for the POWs.

At one point in the war Hitler proclaimed that all airmen

entering Germany by parachute were to be treated as spies and therefore they would be executed. Technically the order was given but was never actually *issued*. Later, in March of 1945, Hitler issued his infamous Nero order, which essentially was a scorched earth policy where everyone would fight to the death and no material of any value would be left intact to be recovered by the allies. It was not stated, but many believe that this implied the execution of all the prisoners of war. No one knows for sure, but what can be said with confidence is that, as Germany and the war itself crumpled to an end, the lives of at least 250,000 allied prisoners were in a *very* precarious position.

There had been speculation that it was Himmler, chief of the SS, who wanted to use the POWs as bargaining chips. There was good reason to believe it was so, but as the end was near, incriminating records were destroyed, so it is unlikely anyone will ever know for sure what the reasoning was, but as 1945 unfolded, a miserable sea of humanity began to march its way across Europe in what was to become the least known major event of World War II.

Whatever the reason, whoever issued the order, it was determined that all of the prisoners held by the Germans should be maintained under German control for as long as possible. They were not to be liberated by the Russians advancing from the east, or the Americans and British advancing from the west.

Stalag Luft 3, which gained fame as the scene of "The Great Escape," was located about 100 miles southeast of Berlin. It was one of the first major camps to be overrun by the Russians. On the night of January 27, 1945 (shortly after the night Dave and Clem were scalding the dog), the 10,000 men of Stalag Luft 3 were marched off to the west to avoid liberation by the Russians. That same night, Clem and his fellow prisoners could also hear the unmistakable sounds of distant Russian artillery in Stalag Luft 4. As January ended the word finally became official. Stalag Luft 4 was also to be evacuated. Those who could not walk very well would be transported by train, and those who could walk would take all their belongings and march off to some unannounced destination. Clem's friend Dave Kimmel had a fairly severe leg wound and opted for the train. He tried to talk Clem into joining him but Clem thought otherwise. There was always the danger of a train being strafed by allied aircraft, and then there was the overriding sense of camaraderie. Shorty and the rest of his friends would make the walk, and Clem just didn't want to leave them. For the last three months they had become his real world, the only life he had, and to leave them right as the war was about to end was just something Clem didn't want to do. Looking back on it now, sixty years later, Clem says, "Man, I thought we would walk for five or six days. If I'd have known it would be three months, I'd have taken that train ride!" (*The story of the train ride is much shorter but only slightly less harrowing than that of the walkers. Their destination was Stalag Luft I, at Barth, Germany. The boxcars were so crowded men could not sit down. At one point they stopped for eight days and both food and water ran out. There were no toilets, ventilation or heat. The train riders have their own incredible horror stories, but everyone is reported to have survived.*)

On February 5, 1945 there was big news at the evening assembly. Early the next day, after morning roll call, they would begin their evacuation of camp. That night before they were to leave, everyone was busy "packing." It really didn't take very long to pack as everyone had so few possessions. A few guys had an extra shirt that they sewed into a rucksack, using the sleeves as straps, but Clem only had one extra pair of socks, an extra shirt and his two blankets that he rolled into a horseshoe and carried on his back. It was still bitterly cold. There was still plenty of snow on the ground and some estimate it was well below zero, so the 10,000 marchers prepared for the cold with all the clothing they could muster. Clem had his wool shirt, military pants, long johns to cover his leg wound, and a second normal set of long johns. He also had a helmet liner, which was a knit cap with a bill, his overcoat, and thankfully, his good pair of shoes. He still walked with a limp, but thanks to his hours and hours of walking in camp he felt he could put in a full day's walk and keep up with the rest of the marchers.

February 6, 1945 dawned cold and crisp. Men fell in for roll call in each of the various lagers to wait their turn for departure. They were full of rumors and excitement after months, or in some cases years, of inactivity. There was clearly apprehension in the air, too, but there was also the realization that the reason for this enormous undertaking was that liberation was not far off. (*At that time the Russian lines were less than 15 miles to the east.*) When it came time for Clem's group they all marched to the administrative vorlager and into a huge warehouse. This enormous warehouse was as large as an airplane hanger. It had large double doors at either end that were thrown open so the prisoners could march right through it. Inside, to the utter disbelief of the marchers, it was stacked to the ceiling with Red Cross food parcels. For months, other than at Christmas, the Germans had been stingy with their distribution of these treasured food parcels. Here before them was the reason why. The Germans had been hoarding them for months and months. To a man, they were downright "pissed!"

As each man marched through he was given one or two food parcels, whatever he thought he could carry. Next, he came to the cigarette bin. The bin was loaded with hundreds of cigarette packs and each man was allowed as many as he could scoop up as he passed by. The men emerged from that warehouse stuffing cigarettes in any pack or pocket they could find. Many had sewn "kangaroo pouches" inside of their overcoats. These, too, were crammed with smokes. As they started down the road their frozen faces were covered with huge grins from receiving the food parcels, nevertheless Clem reports each and every one of them was totally "pissed off" by the thought that all those food parcels had been sitting there all along, as all winter they had been fed crappy bread and rotting potatoes.

Each parcel weighed eleven pounds, so food was stuffed into pockets, sleeves, bandannas, and pouches, anywhere and everywhere that would make it easier than lugging along a heavy box. James Weitkamp from Lager A described it this way:

Now came the first problem: How to march in a column, carrying two relatively heavy boxes even though they contained what was necessary for survival. We were not allowed to stop walking. Some tried to use their blankets to hold their boxes on their backs with pieces of that blanket over each shoulder, or the boxes clutched in their hands in front of their bodies. This didn't work well. I started ripping a box open and started putting the contents into pockets in my pants and overcoat. Then I dropped cans inside my shirt to be held there by my belt. I even tied a piece of rope around my pant legs at the ankle and dropped cans into the inside of the pant legs. None of this worked well and soon became extremely painful. I finally said the hell with it and dropped out of the straggling column and rolled as many cans inside my blanket as I could and tied the roll with the pieces of rope so it could be carried over my shoulder. The first things thrown away were the two cans of margarine. (Clem remembers that this stuff was so bad they would burn it as candles, rather than eat it.) *Having dropped out of the moving group, I naturally ended up much farther back in the column than when I had started. I never again saw any of the men I had been with in the room at Stalag Luft IV.*

Clem's group from Lager B marched about a mile down the road when a whistle sounded and the men were allowed to fall out of formation. Here they began to sort through their parcels and re-pack their new possessions.

The understanding was that this walk was heading to a train station where they would be shipped west and peace was to be negotiated. The next most common rumor was that after a few days they would reach a "sugar factory" where they would be housed until liberation. Whichever destination, it didn't seem to matter, it clearly was just a few days down the road, so guys began to throw out heavy or bulky things they didn't want to carry. Perhaps the commodity most often discarded was the soap. They didn't really need it. The thought of a bath was a joke as they sat there in the frozen mud, so the soap got tossed into the woods. In the long walk ahead they would rue the day, for soap seemed to be the most valuable trading commodity in the eyes of German civilians. They could have traded that soap for a good meal, and starvation was laying in wait for them several hundred miles down the road they were walking.

Once outside of the barbed wire that had defined their existence for the last seven months, the men began to discuss the idea of escaping and making their way east to the Russian lines and liberation. The guard situation was a bit lax. Snow squalls would often cover a dash for the woods, and the security at night was loose. The temptation was real.

The down side of escaping was the Russian army. How could you approach them without getting shot? Their front line troops had a reputation as being the meanest animalistic SOBs on earth. There is a story, believed to be factual, of one such escapee hiding in a barn as the Russians advanced on a German farm. Hiding in the hay, he watched as these front line Russian troops marched the farmer and his wife out into the barnyard, shot them both, butchered them on the spot, and fed them to the hogs.

February 6, 1945: Beginning the death march.
Just up the road the men stopped to rid themselves of unwanted items.

Maybe being a POW marching down a road wasn't such a bad situation. Adding to their dilemma was simply the unknown issue of liberation. Maybe today as they marched down that road they would walk right up on a column of American tanks. Or maybe that would be tomorrow, or the next day. It was obviously going to happen soon and *everyone* in that column knew it, even the guards. Clem reports that by now it was unlikely that the guards would shoot anyone. Everyone on both sides knew that soon fortunes would be reversed. Would a German really want to kill, or even rough up a prisoner, if he knew that next week the guys he was guarding would be the ones with the guns?

So off they marched into the blinding cold of the worst winter of the century.

The first day wasn't too bad. Everyone was well fed and in reasonably good condition. It was just *so* cold that everyone wanted to stop and find a place to warm up. Fortunately they only had to march a few miles that first day when they came to a farm where Clem and his group were allowed to sleep in the barn. Of course the barn couldn't hold the 2000 men from Clem's lager so they were distributed along the road at several different farms. Many German farms have their barn attached right onto the farmhouse. This caused an obvious conflict with the farmer, as he certainly hadn't volunteered his barn for the night. The farmer's main fear seemed to be fire. All of these guys in his hayloft were sure to set the thing on fire and burn it down along with his house. "*Rauchen verboten! Rauchen verboten!*" (No smoking) seemed to be the anthem of every farmer who "hosted" the prisoners. That first night wasn't too bad as everyone had Red Cross food on their menu.

The next morning, as they huddled from the relentless cold, they were given some hot water and managed to make Red

Cross coffee. In a driving snow everyone then fell in shortly after first light. As the guards counted them off, snow and frost piled up on their hats, shoulders and eyebrows. The snow was nearly two feet deep and got into their shoes. Their entire world was white with specks of gray. This miserable little road drifting off into the frozen distance was the only visible feature in their arctic world. It looked as if no matter how long they trudged down that ungrateful little road they would never reach the end, but it headed west.

This was a full day's march and the bitter cold was intense. The dismal gray sky brought criminally cold winds that crept into every seam of their clothing. They did their best to cover every inch of skin, but any exposed part was in danger of frostbite. Despite the continual activity of walking for hours on end, nobody was warm. They put their heads down into the biting wind and just trudged through the snow. There was no train station or sugar factory at the end of the day, just another barn where these unwanted men were packed in. Sleeping in a barn with two blankets in sub zero temperatures is a problem. It's a *big* problem. Many men got little or no sleep. They shivered and shook and huddled together for body warmth. They had no way to wash up and if in the middle of the night they had to relieve themselves they stumbled over bodies and out into a blizzard. It was absolutely awful and it wasn't going to get any better. Day after day, night after night, the same scene repeated itself. A long march. No train station. No sugar factory. Find a barn. Try to survive the night.

The biggest problem next to the cold was the erosion of the Red Cross food supply. Soon there was none, and hunger became an enemy that could be added to the list of miseries. Behind the column of men came a "sick wagon." If a horse or oxen couldn't be requisitioned it would be pulled by about a dozen of the healthy men. If a man couldn't walk that day he wouldn't be left behind. As the days wore on, the sick wagon load increased. So many guys became ill that the load on the sick wagon became impractical. They would often fall out of the column and wait along the road for the sick wagon to arrive. When it finally showed up they would find it so overloaded with guys in far worse situations than they were in, that they just struggled on. As the sick wagon passed through towns or villages the sickest men were often dropped off at whatever medical facilities they had. In the confusion of Germany in 1945, most were never heard from again. Surely some survived and some did not, but records were not kept, names were not known, and their fate will forever be a mystery.

If there was a hero on this miserable march it surely was Dr. Leslie Caplan. Dr. Caplan was given no medicines with which to work but he had the freedom to move up and down this rag tag column and look after the health of the men. He kept an eye on the sick wagon and would do his best to keep up the men's spirits. As the miles ground on he began to see signs of frostbite, trench foot, tuberculosis, pneumonia, and malnutrition. Through all of this human carnage Caplan managed to keep his sense of humor. The following is one of the stories he loved to retell:

Speaking of pneumonia, the technique of listening to a chest was unorthodox since I had no stethoscope. First I would kneel by the patient, expose his chest, scrape off the lice, and then place my ear directly on his chest and listen. After that I would usually remark to the men that if anyone present felt sorry for himself first let him think of my sad case. After all, at one time I used to have lady patients with chest trouble. This was always good for a laugh and a laugh is good therapy.

In the absence of medications, the sick were dosed freely with pep talks. A simple Caplan pep talk would go like this: "The human body is the toughest device ever built, for it is fearfully and wonderfully made. You fellows are young. You are far stronger than you realize. You can take an unbelievable amount of punishment and make a snappy comeback and be as good as ever. Hundreds of men in this column have already done it and you will, too."

The doctor was aware of Clem's leg injuries and did his best to keep an eye on him, but Clem was still managing to limp along at the pace of the column.

This column that consisted of 6,000 to 10,000 men (no one is sure how many there were) began to unravel from day one. It was just impossible to keep that many malnourished men moving smoothly down a road through winter storms, blizzards and freezing cold. At night they were split up and sent to dozens of farms. In the morning they fell in where they were. Maybe they were ahead of their previous place in line, or behind it. No one cared, they just headed west. Often they were lost. The guards were not crack troops but older men who were unfit for front line duties. They were suffering nearly as much as their prisoners. Often at a cross road they would be arguing over a map. They clearly had no set plan other than to head west toward Swinemunde. The line soon stretched out so far that the leaders of the march were a day or two ahead of the tail-enders. Those at the middle or rear of the column soon found themselves sleeping in a barn that the leaders had slept in the night before. At first this caused no problems but within a few days things took a turn for the worse. The men had no supply of water. Very few had any water containers other than cans from their Red Cross parcels. When there was snow they would scoop some up and suck on it as they walked. At night there might be a farmer's well, but as the days wore on it became more and more of a problem as they slogged mile after mile down the road. Soon men were desperate enough to begin drinking from roadside ditches. Then the Red Cross food ran out. On the fifth day out the Germans issued each man a thick slice of bread. That was it. Hunger began to gnaw away as mile after mile burned calorie after calorie. The only way to eat was to scrounge the countryside for potatoes, kohlrabies, or to barter with the locals. Food was eaten undercooked, perhaps raw, and it was seldom clean.

The only thing dirtier than the food was the men themselves. Not only was there little water but there was nowhere to wash. It was so cold that they were wearing every bit of clothing they owned so the idea of "changing" into clean clothes was downright silly. If they weren't tramping through snow they were wading through mud. When they stopped to rest they threw themselves down on the ground in exhaustion. Their clothes became dirty, then filthy, then worse. Lice began to appear. Lack of cleanliness and lice go hand in hand so the little vermin soon were swarming all over this marching mass of incubators. They would pick them off each other and out of their hair. The little beasts wouldn't let men sleep, caused them to continually itch, and in general just made their miserable existence that much worse.

Then people started getting sick.

Within a few days of leaving camp the first cases of diarrhea began to appear. There were NO sanitary facilities on this march and nowhere for the men to wash their hands. At night a sick man would rush out of the barn and let fly wherever he stood. They tried to dig trench latrines every night but the ground was usually frozen and they seldom had shovels.

Floundering around in the dark, men didn't want to stumble into a filled-up trench. They just *went!* That meant that the area around the barns was soon saturated with feces. There was no toilet paper. Men used whatever paper they could scrounge at first, but soon were using snow, leaves, grass, whatever there was, and there was no place to wash their hands afterward. Then the next night another group used the same barn and had to slop through the putrid mess left from the previous night. The poor guys staying there the third night faced a sanitary disaster. Guys were getting covered with the stuff and they brought it back in on their hands and clothes and were sleeping with it. Disease began to spread. Within a few days not only were the men battling cold, hunger and fatigue, now their foe became dysentery. Everyone had it. For the first eight to ten days the guards were eager to keep everyone moving. Somewhere over their shoulders the Russians were to be found advancing up that same road. There are many reports of these sick men not being allowed to step off the road and relieve themselves, so they just ended up soiling their trousers. Soon they were trudging through what became known as *"khaki,"* snow. Little did they know that what lay ahead was over two more months and hundreds of miles of conditions that were only going to get worse. There was no train station, no sugar factory.

After about a week the men reached the Oder River. It is a north flowing river that dumps into the Baltic Sea at Swinemunde. The only way to cross the river was on a barge that was pulled by a tugboat. A couple of days before reaching the river the relentless cold had let up and it had begun to rain. No one had rain gear so their clothes were soon soaked. That meant they only had wet clothes and wet blankets to sleep in at night. During the day it added mud to their misery, but on the afternoon of February 14, the skies began to clear. Normally that would have been a welcomed relief but on this night as the skies cleared the temperature began to plummet. As they were waiting to cross the river the next morning they were all ordered to just camp out in the open. There were no barns on the riverside, just a few trees to offer them protection. The cold that night decided to teach these guys a lesson. The crystal clear air brought out stars by the millions as the temperature kept dropping. It has been reported the temperature that night hit −19 degrees; perhaps it didn't hit that mark but, nevertheless, it was cold enough that many guys feared sleeping. In the kind of cold the marchers experienced that night, men often never wake up as they slip over the edge of consciousness and drift into lethal hypothermia. Clem and Shorty went into the woods and began pulling boughs off of trees. They did their best to build a nest to keep their bodies off the stiffly frozen ground. They had four blankets between them and they hugged together for warmth. They used the blankets to wrap a cocoon around themselves. The cold crept through their blankets and slithered under their clothes. It set both of them to shivering and hugging each other tighter. There was no position that gave them any warmth at all. It was just hopelessly cold, critically cold, lethally cold.

Men reported it was the longest night of their lives. In the morning everything and everybody was covered in a thick white layer of frost. As they began to stir and loosen up frozen limbs they were thankful just to be alive. Despite all of the misery no one had died that night. For all of the suffering that was behind them, and all that lay ahead, every man who survived sleeping on the ground at Swinemunde that night would remember it for the rest of their lives.

For the next couple of days the ferry was busy as it hauled men across the river. On the other side the demeanor of the guards was noticeably better. It then became apparent that this had been their goal, to cross the Oder River before being overrun by the Russians. The guards at last seemed to feel safe, or at least safer, on the western bank of the river. However, the grim realization now sank in. There would be NO train station, NO sugar factory, not tonight, not tomorrow, not *ever*. Everyone now seemed to understand that they were all simply wandering to the west, trying to keep one step ahead of the Russians. It was a depressing reality to conclude that there simply was no final destination for this "Shoe Leather Express." They were so cold and so hungry that it seemed impossible to stagger on, but stagger on they did.

This ferry at Swinemunde had been a choke point where all of the POWs, as well as dispossessed civilians, made their way across the river. Now there appeared to be even less of a destination for this accumulating mass of marchers. The Russian menace, at least for the time being, had been avoided. This miserable mass of freezing, starving men now spread out from Swinemunde and resumed their westward trek down the various roads that led not only to the sunset of each day, but toward the sunset of Germany itself. The question in each man's mind was whether or not it would be the sunset of his own life.

The twin enemies of cold and starvation had come to stay.

It was still mid-February of the worst winter in memory. Any source of warmth was acceptable. The marchers always curled up with their buddies to get through the night. If hay was found in the barns they would do their best to make a nest and insulate themselves from the cold. One of the more sickening accounts of the cold occurred when one of these guys, who was just so bitterly frozen from the day's march in the driving snow, couldn't find any place warm to sleep. He went outside to relieve himself and could feel heat being given off from a decomposing manure pile so he just crawled in it for the night.

Kriegy inventiveness also helped ward off the cold. Someone had discovered how to take a "klim" (milk spelled backward, the cans of milk in the Red Cross parcels) can and, with some metal work, turn it into a little one-burner stove. They even invented a way to cut up tin cans and make them into a squirrel cage fan that could be hand cranked to blow on the few wood chips burning, so the stove would put out considerable heat. Hot water for coffee, tea, or just hot water, was ready in minutes. But food was still a problem.

The Germans tried to find food for the marchers but Germany was now collapsing and it became an "every man for himself" type of situation. In the three months these guys marched, most report there were only one or two Red Cross parcels to be seen the entire time. Sometimes the Germans would find a few potatoes to distribute and they might provide hot water in the morning, but that was it. Calculations done by Dr. Caplan reveal that the average calorie consumption was only 770 per day. They were on their way to starvation, but still they trudged on through the bitter winter.

Most of the nights the guards could find barns for the men. The Germans then set up a perimeter around the farm and the men were often free to roam around within the farm's boundaries and scrounge up what they could. According to Clem, what saved many of the men was the German method of farming. When the potatoes were harvested they were all piled up in mounds out in the fields. The farmers then covered them with straw and dirt to keep them from freezing. As the marchers approached a farm for the night Clem was always on the lookout for the telltale mounds that meant potatoes, and therefore dinner, if you could find a way to slip past the guards. Sometimes they were allowed out of the barn, sometimes they were not. Clem seems to have mastered the art of slinking away in the dark to liberate potatoes or whatever else he could scrounge for a meal.

Clem and Shorty by now were a team that stuck together through thick and thin, but Clem was by far the most adventurous, the most daring of the duo. It worried the dickens out of Shorty, as he was sure Clem would end up getting shot.

One morning Clem and Shorty fell into the line of march directly behind an old wagon that was used to carry all of the packs and belongings of the guards. It was pulled by a couple of oxen and Clem figured that as the Germans took pretty good care of their animals, these oxen were sure to wind up that evening in some place that was warm. If they just followed the wagon all day maybe they could end up with the oxen for the night and get a comfortable night's sleep. The Germans with the wagon seemed like pretty good guys so Clem and Shorty spent the day being as friendly as possible exchanging "stories" as best they could despite the language difficulties. As evening approached they rolled into a little town that had this big barn situated right in the town itself, and sure enough, they rolled the wagon into this big barn with Clem, Shorty, and a bunch of other *kriegies* joining them. It was a huge building and after a while Clem noticed there was a door up at one end of it and guys were crowding in. His developing scrounging skills told him that this accumulation of *kriegies* meant food! In a flash Clem had hopped a fence and pushed his way into what turned out to be some sort of a bakery! The *kriegies* were all waving soap and cigarettes at the girls who worked there, trying to negotiate for a loaf of bread. All of a sudden Clem heard yelling and shouting as the guards came running to break up this attempt at commerce. Clem sized up the situation quickly and knew that when the guards crashed in through the door, bedlam would break loose. He timed it just right and as the attention was turned to the approaching guards he snatched a loaf of bread, hid it under his over coat and threw his back to the wall next to the door. In swarmed the guards and, as they passed Clem, he shot out the door with his warm trophy tucked deep under his arm. That night Clem and Shorty feasted in delight. Sixty years later, still full of pride, Clem says, "And it was pretty good bread. It wasn't any of that old black crap!" As willing as he was to share the prize, all Shorty could say was, "Clem, you're gonna get shot!"

If the farm was of any size at all, and they had hogs, they would also have a big pressure cooker. In the potato mounds, the spuds on the outside were usually frost bitten so these potatoes were then cooked in these big pressure cookers to feed the resulting spud-goop to the hogs. The upshot of this was that those pressure cookers could also be used each morning to boil up hot water for morning brews. Usually that would be tea as the Red Cross parcels had had tea bags. The bags were used over and over and over and over again until they were totally exhausted. Then the *kriegies* would dry out the tea leaves and smoke them! Nothing got wasted.

As his scrounging skills developed, Clem soon learned that any congregation of more than two or three guys meant *food*. He would quickly join the group to reap the rewards of whatever they had discovered. Potatoes, kohlrabies, rutabagas and turnips were about all they could ever find. They then would fire up their little klim-can stove and cook things up, one klim can at a time. Meat was nonexistent. Well almost. The hungrier these guys got, the less likely it was that any animal was to survive their passing. Not many farms still had their dogs after the marchers left. Cats were just as succulent. Nichol and Rennel, in their book *The Last Escape* tell the story of T.D.

Cooke and how he shared a dog with two Russian prisoners of war:

I told them that if they killed it, I would skin and butcher it. They went off and came back five minutes later with the dog. I hacked it up and we partially cooked it in an old boiler, though we barely got it warm because we only had a little fire. But we threw in some carrots and it was a real treat. Another time we ate uncooked rats—raw—and you'd be surprised how good they were.

A real treat was a chicken if one could be caught without German reprisals. A very hungry John Carr told the following account:

One day while on a rest break by a potato field, I dug through the human manure the farmers sprayed over the crops for fertilizer, and got a couple of potatoes for myself and a man named Charles Goud from New York, who looked like he could not go much farther. We cleaned the potatoes the best we could and ate them. I remember that Goud had an Omega watch given him by his wife and he would rather die than trade it for food. Another time, another barn, chickens everywhere! I took a swipe at one as you would a fly. I got her by the neck, put it inside my coat, squeezing like hell so it wouldn't make a sound, praying that the Germans would neither see nor hear the thrashing of the damn thing. I had squeezed so hard, I could not open my hand for some time. They finally put us in the barn. I tried pulling feathers, but the skin came with them. I tried chewing the rubbery uncooked meat as blood ran down my chin, but at least some of the chicken made it to my stomach. Details on that we will omit. Even though I thought this was bad, I heard of one of the men who had bitten off the head of a rat. He was trying to eat the rat when someone pounced on him and took it away.

Then there was a place called Starvation Hill, because after we got to it, we couldn't leave for almost a week, because the roads and rails were under attack by the allies every day, so food was nil. While sitting around the barn one day, I was watching the man beside me picking pieces of flak from his bloody leg, when suddenly he stood up. I looked in his direction and saw two women beckoning him. They each had two pails of hot potatoes they were bringing to the pigs over a little dirt bridge. He, of course, started running toward them with me beside him. Then everyone saw us and came running. In the melee, the women were knocked into the ditch. While we tried to gobble the hot spuds the best we could, one of the women, who was crying, was apologized to by one of the men who could speak Polish. She replied that she wasn't crying because she was hurt or knocked down, but to see men from the richest country in the world groveling for pig food, and that her son who was an American soldier might be doing the same thing at another barn in Germany.

Despite the hunger, the cold, and all of the misery, there were little nuggets of pride or happiness that would occasionally creep into the men's lives. Anthony Capone tells the following story:

It was a day in early March, after spending a night in an open field huddled in groups for protection against the falling snow, that we were again on the road. Today was identical to the many that preceded it. We walked silently in quiet desperation and with a motley demeanor. The only sounds were of shuffling feet, ubiquitous coughing, the occasional shout of a guard and the distant barking of dogs. Unexpectedly, out of the ranks came the feeble sound of someone whistling the Army Caisson Song. It was soon joined by another whistler: "Over hill, over dale..." As more joined in, the German guards yelled to stop but knowing the end of the war was near did not enforce the order with their usual zeal. As others joined in, and the sound grew, and a remarkable thing happened. In one magnificent display of patriotism, the near mile long group of bedraggled kids metamorphosed into a marching unit stepping briskly to the impromptu music with heads high, shoulders back, whistling loudly through puckered lips in formation lines fit for a parade to be viewed by an inspection general. It was a momentary manifestation. It was a grand display which, in our physical condition, could not be sustained. The whistling stopped as spontaneously as it began. The march to Western Germany continued.

    As the men dragged themselves west they found there were some days they simply laid over. For whatever reason, they were given a day or two of rest and were not required to move. For the cold, exhausted men, with blistered feet and dysentery, this was a blessing. The problem, however, was the scrounging for food soon exhausted the few "scroungeable" food resources, so if they spent more than one night in the same place there was nothing at all to eat as they just hunkered down in the barn and waited for the next order to move.

    The hunger was getting worse. Clem was in the minority, having been at Stalag Luft 4 for only three months. Most of the guys had been in POW camps for a year or more. In February when the march began they had already used up all of their body fat, lost a lot of weight, and lived with constant hunger. As

February drifted into March they were famished. All they could think about was food. If they had any personal possessions left it was now time to barter with the locals. For a watch, a ring, or a bar of soap (such as the ones thrown away on that first day), they might be able to buy a loaf of bread from a housewife. Sometimes they could trade cigarettes for something to eat from the Polish slave laborers who were so common on the farms they marched past. It wasn't long, though, until all of their resources for trading were used up. Stricken with crippling dysentery, crawling with lice, freezing to death, on empty stomachs, these men were awakened morning after morning and forced to march ten to twenty miles. Those who lived through it all report that you just can't understand the degradation and inhumanity of it unless you personally lived through it.

As the parade of suffering moved west, the immediate threat of the Russians decreased and the threat of starvation increased. Dr. Caplan reported no deaths due to starvation itself but men were now dying of diseases that they couldn't resist in such a weakened condition. Some felt the only way to escape the misery was to escape from their German captors. Two methods seemed to be favored. The first was to slip out of a barn during the dark of night, avoid the guards, and make for the nearest woods. The second system was to simply find a good place to hide and wait for the marchers and guards to leave the next day. Every morning they counted the *kriegies* but if two or three were missing the Germans never knew if they had slipped away during the night or were hiding somewhere on the farm waiting for everyone to leave.

The first escape attempt that Clem was aware of consisted of a bunch of guys who decided to bury themselves deep in a pile of hay in the upper loft of a barn. Sure enough, the next morning the count came up short. The Germans spread out searching and a couple of guys jabbed at the hay with pitchforks but the escapees were buried too deep to be reached. Clem believes that at this point the Germans didn't want to actually kill their prisoners so one of the guards took out his sten gun and fired a burst of bullets into the air. Rat-A-Tat-Tat. As the bullets sprayed across the wall Clem says those guys came flying out of that hay like gang busters. They all had their hands up and were scared to death. All they got was a good chewing out. Being on this death march was punishment enough.

Another attempt that turned out to be little more than a conspiracy to escape is told by a veteran from Alabama:

Three of us hid in a barn and let the group walk off without us the next day. We stayed hidden until about dusk and then we came out of the barn. The barn had a door at each end. We came out of the barn and were standing in the doorway getting the lay of the land and seeing what direction we should go. I found the North Star and looked to see where the closest woods were. While we were in that end of the barn, two or three children, aged about four or six years old, came in the other end and saw us. But the children very innocently walked down to us. I'm not sure that they knew we were Americans or prisoners until they got down close to us; it was rather dark in the barn. The three of us stood there and speculated about killing those children to keep them quiet and then cutting out and trying to get away. Of course we decided against that. The children left and pretty soon the Germans were out there. They locked us up in the barn, there was a little place there with a wooden door and it even had slats in it, almost like bars on a jail cell. They locked us up in there and then, the next morning, they walked us out. We walked and some kind of slave laborer (a Pole, I think) came out with a brown paper sack and handed it to me and I thought, oh boy, some food, but when I took it, it was awfully light and I opened the thing up and I had about half a sack of tobacco. It was not soft like cigarette tobacco, it was crumbly stuff. But at least you could roll cigarettes out of it, and I did an awful lot of trading to the smokers with that sack of tobacco. So at least I got a little bit out of the escape attempt.

As the men trudged ever westward from their river crossing at Swinemunde their march became ever more meaningless. February drifted into March. They were leaving winter behind, but the disintegration of Germany meant these wandering POWs were a very low priority and food or assistance to them nearly ceased to exist. The German guards provided a few potatoes but mostly food consumption was determined by a man's ability to scrounge. Things were getting critical. Everybody now had dysentery. There were no exceptions. The sick wagon was always at capacity and guys were falling by the wayside. It looked as if the death toll was about to skyrocket when, on March 28, 1945, six weeks after leaving Swinemunde and 53 days after leaving Stalag Luft 4, this emaciated parade of walking skeletons finally reached "The Train Station." They had covered somewhere between 400 –500 miles through the worst winter in memory and now they were at the little town of Ebbsdorf. The men were marched up a siding and at about 3 p.m. they were loaded into freight cars known locally as "40s or 8s." They were designed to hold either 40 men or 8 horses. Of course the number 40 was meaningless now. The guards crammed in more and more men until the car would hold no more. They couldn't even turn around they were packed so tight. The men were given no food, so little water that the can was empty before it was passed halfway through the car, and a single bucket to serve as a toilet. These men now *all* had dysentery. Before the train even started to move some of the guys had to "go." It was absurd to think they could make their way to the bucket so they just ended up soiling their pants. Being packed so tightly they also soiled the guys behind them. Moans of disgust were heard all throughout the car as urine and feces began to soak every man on the train. It was an absolutely disgusting affair that would have plenty of mention in the war crime trials to come.

Mercifully Clem got sick the moment he climbed aboard. His new affliction was the shakes. He began to shake and shiver uncontrollably. Someone went for Dr. Caplan who took one look at him and asked if he had ever had malaria. He had not. There really wasn't anything the doc could do for Clem so they wrapped him in several blankets and forced open a spot wide enough for him to sit down. Clem doesn't recall much about that train ride, due to his delirium, and it probably is best. The guys who do recall, remember a train ride straight out of hell. It lasted for an eternal 33 hours of the most disgusting sanitary conditions possible. They had no food, only sips of water, and little air in this stinking sewage vat of a train car. When they finally stopped and the doors were thrown open, out tumbled a mass of filthy human debris that was unrecognizable as soldiers.

They had reached Stalag 11B, more commonly known as Fallingbostel.

CHAPTER 10
FALLINGBOSTEL

Fallingbostel was huge. Like moths to a flame, Fallingbostel was attracting tens of thousands of emaciated prisoners from all over northern Germany. In groups of dozens or hundreds, or thousands, these legions of dispirited human souls had converged on the abyss of Fallingbostel. Some arrived on the hell trains and were just dumped out like so much human debris. Some straggled in every day after shuffling through snow and mud for hundreds and hundreds of miles. Nobody arrived who hadn't been pushed to the breaking point of human endurance. Bodies were broken, bellies were empty, and morale was nonexistent. It was as if Fallingbostel was Germany's giant city dump and all this worn out, filthy, stinking, unwanted, humanity had just been dumped there.

The camp was not exclusively for airmen or for specific nationalities. There were Russians, Czechs, and Poles as well as American and British POWs. What they all had in common was the same miserable experiences of starvation, disease and absolute physical exhaustion.

If one could have stood above Germany and looked down on the entire country, during that last month of the war, it would have looked as if army ants were swarming across the country from east to west. There were three main flows of POWs. The southern flow is estimated to have had an astonishing 800,000 men. Most of them were Russians, but there were some Americans and British in the mix. To watch that many hungry souls scrounge their way across Germany must have been grim. The middle line of march had "only" 60,000 men trying to keep one step ahead of the Russians. In the north, in Clem's group, 100,000 men were struggling west. That puts the total number close to a million miserable souls who were forced to march, sometimes close to 1000 miles, for no discernable reason. The outcome of the war had already been determined. Additionally, the concentration camps that housed the Jews, gypsies, and homosexuals were now being dumped out on the roads of Germany to endure their own brand of death march. Add to the mix the uncountable number of German civilians who had been successfully "dehoused" and one can see nothing but an army of humanity trudging across the defeated Fatherland.

As the northern marchers straggled into Fallingbostel there soon were over 100,000 prisoners concentrated in this one last camp that was sandwiched between the advancing Russians from the east and the British in the west. It has long been speculated as to why Fallingbostel was seen as the end of the line, the final destination for so many prisoners. The camp, which covered hundreds of acres, was situated a stone's throw from Bergen-Belsen, the notorious death camp where so many Jews were exterminated and cremated in big brick ovens. Many historians have speculated that this was possibly the intended fate of all these POWs. We will never know, as the end-game events of World War II were unfolding so fast that the Nazis were simply losing control of the situation in Germany, not to mention their prisoners of war.

The most distinctive feature of the camp that Clem

remembers was a huge white circus tent that had been erected to house the overflow of marchers that were arriving daily. It was now the first of April so starvation had become a much greater enemy than the cold. There was no way to feed this mass of humanity as the infrastructure of Germany was disintegrating by April of 1945. There were no farms to scrounge, no civilians to barter with. Nothing! Some of the guys under the tent had been captured at Dunkirk! They had been prisoners for five years and were near death's door. Down the road at Bergen-Belsen there were thousands of Jews who had been starved to the point where their pallid skin hung limp on their pathetically frail skeletons. Some of these long-term POWs looked no better. It was heart wrenching to see just how miserable the human condition could become.

After a couple of days Clem began to recover from the train ride and his mind turned of course to food. The only "food" the Germans had served was some water that had been boiled with carrots, turnip skins, and one slice of that awful black bread. Clem, like everyone else, was just *so* hungry. Back at Stalag Luft 4 the mentality of the camp had been "we're all in this together" and things were shared. Now it was "every man for himself" or, as in Clem's case, he and Shorty were a team that would stick together but to hell with anybody else.

By now guys were looking at the forests in the distance and longing to strip the bark off the trees for food. Men had been eating grass and insects as they struggled into camp. On several occasions men reported that they had witnessed starving men actually eat the vomit that their sick comrades had regurgitated. Things were getting critical. Finally Clem decided to see if he could trade some cigarettes for food inside the Russian compound. It was downright dangerous to enter their compound by yourself. An Englishman had gone in there to trade and never returned. Clem rounded up some other traders and they made their way into the world of "Uncle Joe." The Russians just seemed like a different species, animalistic, dirty, dirty, dirty, and mean as hell. It was lucky they were our "friends." In a few minutes Clem emerged with a kohlrabi that he had managed to procure for a few cigarettes. He and Shorty were thankful to have something to eat but he had no desire to do any further shopping at that particular supermarket.

On their third day in camp, the group Clem had arrived with were all lined up and told they were to have a "shower" and be deloused. That caused a low murmur. By now the rumors had begun to spread about Bergen-Belsen, the camp down the road. The concrete fact of concentration camp gassing "showers" was not yet established, but still, there were the rumors. They had left Stalag Luft 4 on February 6 and it was now the first week of April. They had not had a shower in all that time, so why now? Fallingbostel was an end-of-the-line POW camp, not a vacation resort. It all just seemed so very suspicious. The guards marched them up the hill to what looked like a barn that was half sunk into the ground. This didn't look good. They were all ordered to strip naked and throw their clothes on some carts that would be "deloused" while they were in the "shower." Things were getting worse by the minute but what could a guy do? All of these guys were severely weakened from malnutrition, dysentery, and the like. The guards had guns and if you ran for it, they would surely shoot your naked ass.

Each man was given a tiny chunk of soap and these big metal doors creaked open. Clearly the men were resistant, but slowly they inched forward inspecting the "showers" as they went. *Kerslam!* The big metal doors slammed shut. For a moment all was quiet as these quaking naked souls stood frozen with fearful anticipation. All of a sudden the most welcome water any of these men had ever seen in their lives came whooshing out of the showerheads. Praise the Lord! In about fifteen seconds the water stopped and everyone did their best to wash off two months worth of "sweat, slime, and shit." The showers then came on for a few more seconds and the men were released. Hallelujah, it was good to be alive!

Clem says that "The Shower" was the only time from Stalag Luft 4 until liberation that he ever had his clothes off. That one set of clothes had been warmed but was certainly not cleansed of the lice that were living in every garment he owned.

By now the men had time to talk with others about their whereabouts. They had crossed the Elbe River on their march, had noted the names of towns they had passed through, and could pretty much determine just where in Northern Germany they were now located. Things were looking up as everyone realized that the British army led by General Montgomery couldn't be very far to the west. Unfortunately the knock on Monty was that he was a plodder. He was slow to act and was at the absolutely other end of the spectrum from Patton. "Cautious" was the word to describe him, but what these guys all prayed for was a quick strike, and a dash across Germany that would liberate them all. They could visualize British tanks rolling through the gates of the camp and announcing that they were all free.

Any day now.

On April 6, 1945, a week after they had arrived at Fallingbostel, Clem's group was ordered to fall in and told they would now be marching out of camp, back to the *east*, the direction from which they had come. Yes, the British were approaching, so now they must leave.

It is hard to imagine to these bedraggled, starving men, what gawd-awful news that was. It was just *so* unfair. They had survived the death march from start to end, so how could it restart again. For cryin' out loud! It was overwhelming, but off they marched.

By now it was obvious the German command structure was breaking down. All of these groups of men were marched off somewhere back in the direction from which they had come. The British mostly were marched off to the northeast, while Clem and his fellow American marchers headed southeast. Nobody was organizing much food for them anymore so now Clem's scrounging skills became invaluable.

After staggering down the foodless road of starvation for several days, they came to a huge farm with several barns spread all over the place. The Germans posted a perimeter and then turned the men loose inside the farm. One barn had some cement steps going down under the back of it and Clem quickly noticed a bunch of guys scurrying down to what surely must be food. In a flash Clem was down the steps to where he found apples laid out everywhere on big wide shelves. He had on his British battle jacket so he snugged it up tight around his waist and began loading it up with apples. Then he noticed that farther back into the room the guys had torn away some boards and found some unlabeled cans that surely must be food. Men were gathering as many cans as they could carry so Clem hustled back there and got one of the good-sized cans. Just then, one of they guys who was trying to dig in deeper, dumped the entire load of cans and it made a terrible racket. Clem knew that it meant the guards would be there on the run, so again he hustled back to the door, hid behind a tractor wheel, and when the guards rushed in he scooted out the door with his treasures. He got back to Shorty who exclaimed, "You're gonna get us shot!" and then they hurriedly stashed their goodies in a haystack as the guards were sure to come searching.

It wasn't long before all the prisoners were ordered to fall in, outside, in front of a big tree. Tied with their backs to the tree, were two of the can thieves who had been caught in the act. In a stern voice, the leader of the guards announced that the prisoners were welcome to keep any of the apples they had found but they absolutely must return the cans. If they did not return the cans and fill that big cart by morning, the prisoners tied to the tree would be shot.

Clem reports that by now they absolutely knew that this was a bluff. With the British on their heels, there was just no way the guards would execute these guys, but the next morning every single can was returned to the cart. During the night Clem and Shorty dug up their treasure and started in on their apple supply. Next they managed to open their prized can. Disappointingly it was just filled with broth and a layer of lard on top, but they ate it anyway. During the night, Clem then snuck out and returned the can as he had been ordered to do. So did everybody else. They followed their orders, and sure enough, the next morning, as ordered, all the cans were on the cart. There sat an entire cartload of *empty* cans.

Nobody got shot.

About a week after they had started to back track on this endless march, the prisoners were spending the early morning building little fires around this farm so they could boil some water to cook up the seed potatoes they had dug up the night before. The day was April 12, 1945. They heard a commotion and noticed this high-falutin' German with britches and boots come swaggering through camp and just raising hell. With his cane, he was knocking over cans of water and stirring up the little fires. From time to time he would whack one of the men on the back and would make derisive comments to them. The asshole was really having himself a good time. He approached the fire Clem was at, took one swing at their water and chortled derisively, *"Roosevelt ist tot, Roosevelt ist tot!"* (Roosevelt is dead, Roosevelt is dead!) and went prancing away to harass the other marchers.

The news sent a pall over the already beaten group of men. How could it be, when they knew the war was almost over? Roosevelt was their father figure. He was the only president most of these young men had ever known. How could he possibly be gone now when the war was so close to its conclusion?

They each had their little chunk of potato and began their march east with heavy hearts that day.

As the British squeezed in from the west, one of the obvious signs of their proximity was all of the air action. Every day now, fighters could be seen patrolling the skies looking for "targets of opportunity." Anything that moved was in danger of being strafed by these low flying flyboys. By now the pilots were aware that many of these lines of humanity marching the roads of Germany were allied POWs. Some of the guys down there on the ground were their friends.

During April, Clem and Shorty awoke one morning to the sound of fighter planes overhead. The dilapidated barn they were in was filled with straw and a few old rusting pieces of farm machinery. As they lay there they followed the friendly sound of the British planes as they circled overhead. The roar of the spitfires diminished as they passed the barn and flew on down the valley. All at once, the men sat up in horror as they recognized the unmistakable sound of the planes turning around and diving down to make a strafing run. As Clem and Shorty dove under an old tractor the machine guns cut loose and the planes screamed overhead. Men were piled under that machinery like cordwood as the bullets tore through the barn.

Wood bits, hay, hats, shoes, everything loose went flying, but when they came up for air everyone had escaped the carnage. Not everyone was so lucky. Unfortunately mistakes were made, and POW deaths due to "friendly fire" occurred. The British had an especially draconian day when their bedraggled column of marchers was strafed by some of their own planes killing some 60 men in one of the saddest incidents of the entire war.

Sometimes these British planes would find a column of retreating Nazis to attack and they would really give them hell. The up side of this was that by now what was left of the German army was using anything it could to move men and equipment, even horse-drawn wagons. When these fighters shot up such a convoy it was not unusual for them to kill some of the drought animals that were hauling the wagons.

Sad as that might be for the animals, it was a bonanza beyond belief for the POWs if they came upon a recent kill. Numerous stories are told by these veterans how they felt they couldn't walk another mile when they came around a corner and there lay a dead horse. Hallelujah! They all fell out of line and the horse would be butchered and eaten on the spot.

Now they were continually joined on the road by civilians going in all directions. Germany was on the move as the allies closed in. The guards got kinder all of the time and every once in a while one of them would just disappear. By now everyone was looking out for his own skin. Knowing the British were close on their heels, escape attempts were becoming more common. It wasn't so cold now, so men felt that if they could survive on their own for a few days, and make their way to the British lines, or just hunker down and wait to be overrun by the British, they would be free. It wasn't unusual for the morning roll call to be short a guy or two. Deadly threats were still being made but it seemed unlikely that anyone would actually get shot.

Clem, the daring scrounger, now turned his thought to escape. He knew that trying to talk Shorty into it was useless. Shorty would be afraid they would be shot! Instead, Clem buddied up with Eddie Dobrun, a fellow risk taker who was from Toledo, Ohio. Eddie spoke some Polish, so that might be of help as there were a lot of Polish slave laborers still under German control.

As April wore on they began to hear artillery from the west. That was a really good sign, as they knew the British had to be within twenty miles. Clem and Eddie were tired of marching, tired of starving, tired of German guards, and tired of the war. They decided the time was right to make their get-away and find those British lines. As dusk settled in one evening Clem and Eddie snuck out of the barn and crept down to a little lean-to where they waited for dark. Clem's overcoat looked way too military so he cut off the bottom several inches, in hopes of making it look more civilian. A Polish lady saw them in the lean-to and brought them Polish pancakes. Often the Poles were sympathetic to the plight of the marchers and this kind lady was no exception. Not knowing when they would have their next meal, and being starved to start with, they kept wolfing down the pancakes as fast as they could. At last it was dark. They were on somewhat of a hillside and there was a big plowed field below them and then a village below that. They waited for the guard to pass, then began creeping across this big field. They successfully made the crossing, then settled down again to reassess their situation. Their next objective was to bypass this village and head on down the hill. They swung wide around the town and then to their horror they came upon a set of railroad tracks.

At this point in the war, railroads were heavily patrolled so this was a serious impediment to their get-away. They hunkered down in the bushes to watch what was going on and finally decided that they could make a dash for a culvert that ran under the tracks, and once inside the culvert they would be safe. Clem went first. He still was limping but was highly motivated to be quick. He dashed across and all was well. Now it was Eddie's turn. He got about halfway across when he heard a guard shout and a dog began to bark. As he scurried into the culvert he could hear the dog racing along the gravel, then OUCH, it had him by the ass! The escape was over. At first they feared they might be shot, but soon they realized these railroad guards didn't want to kill anyone; instead they just made them run the two miles or so back to the barn.

As they came huffing and puffing back into the barn Shorty wanted to know where they had been. When they responded his only comment was, "Clem, you're gonna get shot!" There was no punishment from the Germans that night but Clem had one of the worst nights of the entire death march. The combination of running back and the pile of Polish pancakes in his gut was more than he could handle. He spent the entire night sicker than a dog. That was punishment enough.

The escape attempt wasn't the only pickle that Eddie got Clem into. Perhaps it was Clem's fault, too, but these two guys were a daring duo.

One night they were in a little barn that was attached up over a farmhouse. Eddie woke Clem and said, "Let's sneak out and have a smoke." They crept down to a landing where there wasn't any straw and began to share a cigarette. They were leaning against a locked door when Eddie started sniffing the air. "Hey, Clem, do you smell that, I think I smell food!" whispered Eddie. The locked room was right over the kitchen, so as Clem stood watch, Eddie went to work on the lock. Eddie had skills. In a few minutes Clem heard the lock fall open and he and Eddie took a peek inside. Holy cow!!! The little room was full of hams hanging from the rafters, and slabs of bacons lying on a table. As they started toward their bounty the floor creaked something awful, but what the heck, in for a penny, in for a pound. Clem cut down a small ham. Eddie helped himself to a slab of bacon, and they scuttled back to the hayloft. This was a true treasure. The trouble was that if the food was discovered as missing, these treasures really could bring on some serious consequences. Neither Clem nor Eddie could sleep at all that night as they worried about the treasures in the hay. Hour after hour they kept imagining just how good this real food, this real meat, would taste. In the middle of the night their hunger got the best of them. They hauled out the ham; each took a couple of slices and stuffed it back in the hay. The morning might bring all hell down on them, but for now this was better than Christmas. No Christmas ham would *ever* taste that good.

In the morning, when Shorty was awakened, Clem whispered, "I have something to show you."

"Jeeeesus Christ," yelped Shorty, as Clem produced the ham. "You're gonna get us shot, Clem."

They soon fell in for morning roll call with the golden ham wrapped in Clem's blankets. Clem waited fearfully for the ax to fall. Everyone was accounted for so they were all told to face east and they were off. The ham caper had succeeded. *Man*, thought Clem, *I'm gonna have some serious trading material*, and he did.

By now every man who had participated in this death march and survived, had lost at least 1/3 of his body weight. Many of these guys, who were in their early twenties and in excellent shape when captured, now weighed less than a hundred pounds. Clothes hung on skeletal frames. Cheekbones were protruding and everybody's ribs were showing. It was just absurd that after eighty-some days on the road they were still being forced to march. Clearly it was just a matter of days, but orders were orders, and the guards moved this pathetic column of the walking dead ever eastward.

It was May now, and one morning Clem awoke to a terrible pain in his bad leg. He unwrapped his long johns and was horrified to see what a stinking mess it had become. Someone went for Dr. Caplan, who soon was busy cleaning up the mess with a wet rag. A piece of the shrapnel that was still imbedded in Clem's leg had worked itself loose and migrated to the surface where it had broken through. The resulting mess was getting infected and alarmed Dr. Caplan. He reached in and extracted the chunk of steel, cleaned it all up the best he could, wrapped the leg back up, and announced, "Son, you're through walking, how on earth did you ever walk this far on such a leg?"

Clem had walked about 600 miles since February 6th. He had endured the death march and now it was time for him to just wait for liberation. Dr. Caplan put him and a couple of other invalids in an old ox-cart and was about to send him to town when it hit both Clem and Shorty that they were about to go their separate ways. Shorty was in disbelief. They had visualized their mutual liberation and surely it wasn't far off. To have come this far and be separated broke their hearts. It just wasn't right. To this day, sixty years later, you can see in Clem's eyes that it was a tough separation. It is hard to imagine any event in life that could bond two men as closer friends than the experience, the food, the miseries, the body heat, the disappointments, and the miles that these two guys had shared. They said their "goodbyes," and Clem was off in the cart. They would never again see each other.

A couple of miles down the road the cart rattled into a town and stopped at a makeshift little "hospital" that had previously been a service station. There were no doctors around, but sick and injured guys were being warehoused there until the war was over. They had spread straw on the floor to make themselves comfortable but automotive posters and calendars still adorned the walls. Clem found a place in the rear of the building and made himself comfortable in the straw. He slept most of that day and the next.

By now it seemed common knowledge that the British were "just down the road." Most of the German guards at the "hospital" had simply melted away into the civilian population. The few who stayed were the kind ones, the thoughtful ones, and they were making sure everyone had enough food and water. They knew only too well that their lives were about to change as dramatically as were those of their prisoners.

On May 5, his second morning there, Clem was resting in the rear of the hospital/service station when he heard the unmistakable sound of military vehicles grinding down the road. Everybody who could stand got up and began to look down the road, praying that these were British vehicles and not the German army making one last stand. Hearts sank as the telltale clanking of tank treads could be heard. The last thing they needed now was to be caught in the middle of some last-ditch battle. All of a sudden screams of jubilation erupted through the little service station. The lead tank carried that lovely Union Jack! Those beloved British Tommies piled out and announced, "Congratulations, for you lads, the war is over!"

Yes indeed. After 3 years, 29 bombing missions, 9 months as a POW, 88 days and 600 miles of marching, for Clem Pine, the war was over.

CHAPTER 11
LIBERATION

Liberation! It was almost too good to be true. As soon as the cheering and hugging was over the reality of it all began to sink in. It was *over*! There would be no more marching, no more starving. The sense of freedom washed through the little service station and out onto the road. Although everyone in the little hospital was injured, some of the guys could walk. No sooner had the reality of their freedom set in than they began walking down the road to town. In no time at all they were back with eggs, real bread, schnapps, anything and everything they could find. The tables had turned and now it was their turn to demand whatever they wanted.

Clem's leg was still oozing somewhat and kept him from joining the treasure hunt in town. It was such a relief to just be liberated that he really didn't mind missing the town side adventure. Within hours the British came in and doused him from head to toe with DDT to rid him of his outer layer of lice, fed him, and packed him into an ambulance. The trip out of Germany lasted about a day, ending about 250 miles to the southwest in Liege, Belgium, where he was sent to recuperate from his wound.

At Liege there was a big, beautiful, clean hospital, but Clem was so absolutely filthy the nurses were not about to allow him onto their premises. He had been 88 days on the march with only that one15-second shower at Fallingbostel a month before. He stunk.

Showers, hot showers, were set up across the road for these stinking marchers. A big, broad smile creeps across Clem's face today as he recounts the feeling of those long, hot, soapy showers as he and his fellow POWs languished in the luxury of it all. After a total scrub down they had a shave and a haircut, followed by crisp, clean pajamas and a luxuriant maroon robe. Clem still couldn't walk very well so he was put into a wheel chair and wheeled across the street where he and his cleanliness were now welcomed into the antiseptic hospital.

Understandably, what Clem desired most was not food, it was to be warm and clean. He had learned to survive on scant food but he had never gotten used to being so cold and filthy, so a nice warm bed in that clean hospital was all he could ever have wished for.

Within a few days he was walking again and was allowed out to explore the city. His first recollection is ice cream. What a treat after those months and months of scrounged, disgusting meals. By the end of May he was sitting at sidewalk cafes, sipping beer, and watching the girls go by. Life can be just so glorious!

Soon he was sent off to the coast of France where he waited in a camp to be shipped back home. He had a pass to go to Paris, enjoyed the wine, and within a couple of weeks boarded a liberty ship bound for The United States of America.

Summer was coming on now so it was a delightful trip of sleeping on deck, making new friends, and swapping war stories. Through it all there was just one negative aspect of this joyous liberation that Clem had so long dreamt about. Clem had been separated from his buddies.

Through those months in Stalag Luft 4 and the 88 days on the death march, Clem, Shorty, Dave Kimmel and a few others had formed such a tight bond that they were sure they would be friends forever. They had plans to get together after the war to have a few beers, eat some great meals, meet each other's families, and tell their stories. It was not to be.

When most of the men finally got home after World War II in Europe they were so happy to see their families and old friends that somehow many wartime buddies got lost in the shuffle. They lived all over the country and were busy picking up the pieces of their own lives, too. Clem had a letter from Shorty and exchanged a couple of letters with Dave Kimmel but he never saw either of them again.

The guys in the Eighth Air Force did organize reunions and the 351st got together, but it was many years later. There has never been a reunion for the thousands of men who walked the incredible Nazi Death March of World War II.

EPILOGUE/ AUTHOR'S COMMENTS

The Least Known Major Event of World War II
According to Nichol and Rennell in their thorough book *The Last Escape – The Untold Story of Allied Prisoners of War in Europe 1944-45,* nearly a million men were on the frigid march as the winter of 1945 descended upon Europe. The story of Clem Pine is certainly no different than that of thousands upon thousands of others, and yet until Nichol and Rennell published their book in 2002 the story has almost never been recorded. Joe P. O'Donnell has self published *The Shoe Leather Express*, a fascinating collection of stories, remembrances, and poems concerning POW life and the death march across Europe. Additionally, a few personal accounts can be found on the internet. Other than these rather rare publications, this amazing story has seldom found its way into print. Even harder to

believe is the fact that this event is never portrayed in the movies or on TV. We have all seen films on D-Day, The Battle of the Bulge, The Bataan Death March, the campaigns in North Africa and Italy, even The Great Escape from Stalag Luft III, but there is almost *nothing* on the European Death March.

For the past two years, I have interviewed numerous World War II veterans concerning this project. Unless they participated in the death march, even the veterans themselves have had no knowledge of this incredible ordeal. I have repeatedly asked myself, "Why?" How could such a major event involving so many men have been totally ignored? Of course I have no answer, but I do have some thoughts concerning the lack of "publicity" concerning this awful forced march.

The European war ended in early May for these poor souls who had been on the march for so many months, and of course it officially ended May 8, 1945, "VE Day." The papers were full of victory, of heroics, and the thoughts of our boys coming home. It was a time for celebration, not a time to dwell on what our POWs had been through. And it must be remembered that the war was not over. The war in the Pacific was still being fought. The battle for Okinawa was still underway, so the unfortunate story of the plight of our European prisoners of war was lost in the events raging in the Pacific.

It also should be remembered that no matter how inhumanely the allied prisoners had been treated in POW camps and on the death march, it paled in comparison to what was discovered as the allies liberated the various Jewish concentration camps and extermination camps scattered around Europe. Those hauntingly horrific photographs and movies of the ghostly Jewish survivors are just so emotionally charged that they become permanently imbedded in the mind of anyone who has ever seen them. When that Nazi sickness was first revealed to the world at large there was such an outrage, such an overpowering disgust, that obviously our men who had been through their own miseries were not about to step forward and say, "Hey, we suffered, too." Ugly though the Nazi Death March had been, it certainly was not comparable to the horror the Jewish people of Europe had suffered, so the story just went untold.

The other factor that must be considered in the silence surrounding the death march is the men themselves. These men had been through physical and emotional hell. They were so starved, filthy, and emotionally beat up that all they wanted to do was clean up, eat, and go home. Surviving a death march is not something that makes a guy proud. It makes him thankful. For months these men had been forced to become thieves in order to steal enough food to survive. An "every man for himself" attitude developed where each guy just took care of himself and his immediate buddy. It was not a heroic event as much as it simply was an effort to survive. There was no unit pride, no "Band of Brothers." There was only survival.

It is interesting to note that Clem Pine spent more time as a prisoner of war than he did as a member of the 351st bomb group, and although he has been to many reunions of his bomb group there has never been a reunion for the prisoners of war. It seems as if the men just did not care to recall those days and dredge up those memories, and yet the days in England with their buddies, chasing girls, and beer, and Germans, are being relived over and over again as the old vets gather annually to celebrate the seminal event in each of their lives.

Why Did the Germans Conduct the Death March?
This question has not only been asked by historians but

surely it must have been asked by each and every man who participated in the march. It wasn't just Stalag Luft 4 but virtually every prison camp the Germans operated was emptied out as the Russian front approached from the east. The men were marched west, and then, as in Clem's case, sometimes they were marched back to the east, retracing their steps. This obviously took German manpower and at least some resources, and in the end they gained nothing from it. So why did they do it? Had the Russians been allowed to simply overrun the camps and liberate the men it might actually have benefitted the Germans, as the Russians would then have had the responsibility of feeding and caring for these hundreds of thousands of men. Nearly all the prisoners were in such poor physical shape by liberation that they could not have immediately taken up arms against the Germans, and presumably their care and feeding might have slowed the Russian advance, even if the effect was minimal. So why did the Germans do it?

It was rumored throughout the war that Hitler had issued an order to have all of the POWs executed. It is doubtful that such an order was actually produced, as the issue of reciprocity always arose. What would the allies do to the German POWs if the allied prisoners were executed?

After the assassination attempt on Hitler in June of 1944 things within the German high command were rearranged. Himmler, the dreaded chief of the SS, was to oversee the prisoner camps from that time on. According to Nichol and Rennell, "Himmler planned to survive Hitler, make peace with the Americans and British, and emerge at the end as his country's leader." If that is true, it may be that Himmler planned on using the POWs as bargaining chips that could be used in some sort of end game deal making.

The truth is that nobody really knows for sure. What seems to be the case is that the lives of these men were in a more precarious position than they may have known. One angry order from the Fuhrer and none of them might have come home.

Big Stoop

The Story of Clem Pine and the rest of the men of Stalag Luft 4 cannot end without a few comments concerning the fate of Big Stoop.

As the accounts emerge of life in Stalag Luft 4, and the death march that followed, the one person who always generates stories is Big Stoop. He was universally despised by the men for being so outright mean. He was a huge man and used his bulk to bully, intimidate, and abuse prisoners who were helpless in his presence. In no account that I have found has anyone ever uttered a kind word about the man. As the POWs put it, "He was a real bastard."

When liberation finally arrived and the men gathered in camps waiting to be sent home, the final story of Big Stoop was finally told. Perhaps.

Clem recalls that he heard "first hand" from a guy who witnessed the scene, upon being set free, the guys who were guarded by Big Stoop immediately took their revenge on him. Their first act of liberation was to hang him from a flagpole!

A veteran from Alabama relates the tale in his memoirs, that he saw five hated Germans lying dead on the road with their faces shot all to pieces. One of them was Big Stoop.

Joe O'Donnell reports *two* stories concerning the fate of Big Stoop. The first was that he was "found in a roadside ditch with a hatchet imbedded into his skull, mightily dead." The second claims, "Two liberated American prisoners of war were carrying a copper oval canning kettle. When asked what they had in the kettle, they proudly displayed Big Stoop's head. Absolutely dead."

No one *really* seems to know what happened to Big Stoop but all of the accounts of his death are so gruesome that it is safe to say that if the *kriegies* caught him during liberation his fate must have been ugly. Whether or not any of these stories are true, or if they are all just wishful thinking, it doesn't seem to matter. When the war ended it appears that, in the eyes of the *kriegies*, Big Stoop got what he deserved.

Life After the War

When Clem Pine arrived home after the war it didn't take him very long to find a wonderful woman and make her his bride. Clem married Ann in 1945 and within a few years along came Becky, Steven, Grant, and Harlan. His career in the Air Force took him to Taiwan, Japan, Thailand, and finally to Klamath Falls, Oregon, where he retired in 1970. Along the way he and Ann enriched their family by adopting Lynne, their Chinese daughter, and Kim, their Korean son. They also became foster parents to Don, their Native American foster son.

It is harder to imagine a finer American family than the Pines. Getting to know Clem as he shared his journey through World War II has been an absolute pleasure. He has certainly taught me why he and those just like him deserve to be called, "The Greatest Generation."

Yes, thank you, Clem Pine. It is an honor to know you.

Clem Pine with a B-17.

Clem Pine at the business end of a B-17. 2003.

BIBLIOGRAPHY

Bailey, Ronald H. and the Editors of Time-Life Books, *The Air War in Europe*. Chicago: Time-Life Books, 1981.

Bradley, James, *Flyboys*. Boston: Little, Brown and Company, 2003.

Bowman, Martin W. *Castles In The Air*. Washington, DC: Brassey's, 2000.

Cadin, Martin, *Black Thursday*. New York: Dell, 1960.

Caldwell, Donald L, *JG 26 Top Guns of the Luftwaffe*. New York: Ivy Books, 1991.

Freeman, Joseph, *The Road to Hell – Recollections of the Nazi Death March*. St. Paul, Minnesota: 1998.

Freeman, Roger A. *The Mighty Eighth – A history of the U.S. 8th Army Air Force*. Garden City, NY: Doubleday and Company, 1970.

Flyer, Carl, D.D.S. Major (R) – AF, Staying *Alive*. Leavenworth, Kansas: 1995.

Gunston, Bill, *The Illustrated Encyclopedia of Combat Aircraft of World War II.* New York, New York: Salamander Books, 1978.

Hammel, Eric, Air War Eurpoa, *America's Air War Against Germany in Europe and North Africa, Chronology, 1942-1945.* Pacifica, California: Pacifica Press, 1994.

Jablonski, Edward, Flying Fortress, *The Illustrated Biography of the B-17s and The Men Who Flew Them.* Garden City, NY: 1965.

Miller, Francis Trevelyan, Litt.D., LLD. *War In Korea and The Complete History of World War II,* Great Britain: 1955.

Nichol, John and Tony Rennell, *The Last Escape – The Untold Story of Allied Prisoners of War In Europe 1944 – 1945.* NY, Viking: 2002.

O'Donnell, Joseph P. *The Shoe Leather Express February 6, 1945 To May 2, 1945.* Triangle Reprocenter of Hamilton: 1982.

Willmott, H.P. *B-17 Flying Fortress.* Secaucus, NJ: Chartwell Books, 1980.

CPSIA information can be obtained at www.ICGtesting.com
Printed in the USA
LVOW08s1320091013

356168LV00001B/14/P